Study and Revise

GCSE French

Caroline Woods

Acknowledgements

The author and publishers would like to thank the following for the use of material in this publication:

EDEXCEL London Examinations – Modern Foreign Languages: French in Chapter 1 **p. 10** Higher Task 1; ***L'Indépendant*** no. 192 August 10, 1996 in Chapter 6 **pp. 45–46** Higher Task 3; ***Okapi* Presse Bayard** no. 569 'Portez-vous des vêtements de marque?' September 23, 1995 in Chapter 7 **p. 55** Higher Task 1, no. 581 March 23, 1996 'Ça c'est du sport' in Chapter 12 **p. 123** Reading Higher Exercise 2; ***Phosphore* Presse Bayard** November, 1995 in Chapter 12 **p. 117** Listening Higher Exercise 3, July–August 1996 in Chapter 12 **p. 124** Reading Higher Exercise 4; ***Mikado* Milan Presse** April, 1996 in Chapter 12 **p. 123** Reading Foundation/Higher Exercise 3.
AQA: Reading Specimens 2003 Higher Tier, Exercise 6 (Strasbourg) in Chapter 12 **p. 124** Reading Higher Exercise 3.
OCR: Speaking Specimens 2003 Speaking Test Section 3 Card 5 in Chapter 12 **p. 118–119** Speaking Higher; Reading Specimens 2003 Section 1, Exercise 4 (Camping du Soleil) in Chapter 12 **p. 121** Reading Foundation Exercise 4.

Every attempt has been made to obtain the required permission.

First published in this edition 2004
exclusively for WHSmith by
Hodder & Stoughton Educational
338 Euston Road
London NW1 3BH

Impression number 10 9 8 7 6 5 4 3 2
Year 2010 2009 2008 2007 2006 2005

Illustrations: Kath Baxendale, Karen Donnelly, Rebecca Hutchins, Andrea Norton, John Plumb, Dave Poole, Katherine Walker

Prepared by *specialist* publishing services, Milton Keynes

Printed and bound in the UK by Scotprint

A CIP record for this book is available from the British Library

ISBN 0 340 85867 2

Contents

Tackling the tiers without the tears 1

1 Moi 7
- Foundation 7
- Test yourself 8
- Higher 9
- Test yourself 10

2 Chez moi 12
- Foundation 12
- Test yourself 14
- Higher 15
- Test yourself 17

3 Mes passe-temps 18
- Foundation 18
- Test yourself 21
- Higher 22
- Test yourself 23

4 En vacances 24
- Foundation 24
- Test yourself 27
- Higher 30
- Test yourself 31

5 Mes vacances 33
- Foundation 33
- Test yourself 35
- Higher 37
- Test yourself 39

6 En ville 40
- Foundation 40
- Test yourself 42
- Higher 44
- Test yourself 45

7 On fait des achats 47
- Foundation 47
- Test yourself 51
- Higher 53
- Test yourself 55

8 Au café / Au restaurant 56
- Foundation 56
- Test yourself 58
- Higher 62
- Test yourself 63

9 Au collège 66
- Foundation 66
- Test yourself 68
- Higher 69
- Test yourself 70

10 Au travail 72
- Foundation 72
- Test yourself 74
- Higher 75
- Test yourself 77

11 Word lists 78

Summary 78
1 **Moi** Foundation + Higher 79
2 **Chez moi** Foundation + Higher 82
3 **Mes passe-temps** Foundation + Higher 85
4 **En vacances** Foundation + Higher 89
5 **Mes vacances** Foundation + Higher 91
6 **En ville** Foundation + Higher 94
7 **On fait des achats** Foundation + Higher 96
8 **Au café / Au restaurant** Foundation + Higher 100
9 **Au collège** Foundation + Higher 103
10 **Au travail** Foundation + Higher 104
The international world 105
General 108
Grammar 109
- Perfect tense 109
- Present tense 110
- Future tense 112

Time 113

12 Mock exam paper 114
- Before you start 114
- **Listening** Foundation 114
  - Foundation + Higher
  - Higher
- **Speaking** Foundation 118
  - Foundation + Higher
  - Higher
- **Reading** Foundation 120
  - Foundation + Higher
  - Higher
- **Writing** Foundation 125
  - Foundation + Higher
  - Higher

Contents

13 Grammar **127**

Verbs 127

Nouns 134

Adjectives 135

Adverbs 137

Pronouns 138

Index **140**

Tackling the tiers without the tears

How do I use this book?

This *Study and Revise GCSE French* book covers ten topics. Each chapter is divided into two tier sections: Foundation and Higher. A numbered checklist at the beginning of each section lists the things you should know for each tier within that chapter. Use the checklist by shading in the Fine or Help! buttons as you work through your revision to keep a record of your progress and to identify where you need to concentrate your efforts. You will also see how your memory and skills are growing.

The chapters contain the vocabulary and structures that you need to achieve good GCSE grades for any of the exam awarding bodies. The language is presented in a way that is easy to follow and remember.

Find out from the start which tiers you have been entered for so that you can see which sections of the book will be most useful to you. For example, if you were entered for all the Higher papers except in Writing, you would work through all the Foundation and Higher chapters but you could leave out the Higher tasks marked with the Writing symbol. In this way, you will be able to make the most of your revision time.

Use the Checklist and the Notes/Options

Work through each chapter at your own pace: shade in the **Checklist** (**Fine/Help!**). For all of the items that you have ticked Help! go on to read the **Notes/Options** on that point.

Then move on to the **Test yourself** tasks which include exercises within the four skills (Listening, Speaking, Reading, Writing); these will help you to recall the content of the chapter and to give you some exam practice. Remember, always mark your answers using the upside-down key. If your answer is not satisfactory, look back at the Notes/Options on the points that have troubled you.

Before moving on from one chapter to the next, you should look back at the Checklist to be certain that you are confident with all of the items on the list. You should have shaded all of the Fine buttons before you move on.

A practice mock exam

Finally, there is a mock exam in Chapter 12. It is a full mock exam for Listening, Speaking, Reading and Writing. Work through the tier which you intend to tackle in the exam for each exam part.

A grammar reference

You will find the grammar explanations in Chapter 13 very useful as your revision progresses.

Please write on me! Make notes as you go, using highlighter pens. This is one book on which you can make your 'mark'! Feel free to make notes to yourself in the book. Keep blank paper and coloured pens by you as you revise for use when you want to. Revising should be an 'active' use of time so that you remember more effectively!

Train your memory

Your memory improves the more you use it – according to scientific research! Realise that you cannot leave all of that French revision until the night before your exam – there just won't be enough time!

Plan out the time before your French exam so that you revise a little every day, allowing your mind to absorb the information. Give more time to the topics that you find most difficult. Bear in mind the other subjects you are taking and juggle your revision time carefully.

Some people find that they are most receptive to learning and memorising in the mornings, but only you can decide what works best for you. Be aware of what are the hardest topics and structures for you, and don't leave them to the last minute!

TOP TIPS for learning vocabulary

1 Use different coloured pens to highlight masculine and feminine words.

2 Draw an item or symbol for key vocabulary.

3 Don't try to learn more than ten words at a time.

4 Use a list of ten words, start at the bottom and work upwards, as well as downwards.

5 Visualise each item of vocabulary as you say the word in French.

6 Record yourself – play it back and imagine the item again.

7 Ask friends, brothers, sisters or parents to test you on vocabulary.

8 Remember that with regular effort you can build a bigger vocabulary and recall it.

9 Think positive. Vocabulary is the key and the more often you learn small chunks, the easier it gets.

Are you sitting comfortably?

You need to be at ease when you are revising. Here are some tips to help you choose an ideal working environment.

LOCATION Never revise in the kitchen or the living room with the TV on or with brothers or sisters around. Find a place that is quiet and where there are no distractions. If you find it hard to revise at home, you could go to your library.

LIGHTING Natural light is best. If you can, sit by a window. If you have to work in artificial light, try to use a lamp rather than fluorescent lighting as this can give you eye strain. Avoid shadows; make sure that the light comes from your left if you are right-handed, and from your right if you are left-handed.

HEATING If you are too warm while you are revising, you might find that you start falling asleep – not ideal for training your memory! Fresh air helps concentration so open the windows while you are working, or at least during your short breaks.

SPACE Organise your desk or table so that your books, notes, dictionaries, pens and paper are within easy reach. If you have to keep getting up to look for things you will be easily distracted.

POSITION Make sure your chair is at the right height and keeping your back straight while you are revising. You might get back-ache if you sit awkwardly. Never work in an armchair or lying on your bed: you will be too relaxed to take much in!

FUEL Meals are very important. Pay as much attention to your food intake as does an athlete training for a competition! Limit the amount of sugary and fatty things you eat as these increase irritability and can disrupt concentration. Likewise, stimulating drinks (such as coffee and tea) can revive you in the short term, but they might also disturb your sleep pattern and affect your memory if you're tired.

Which exams will I be taking?

For your GCSE French exam, if you are following an AQA (Specification A), EDEXCEL, OCR or WJEC course, you will be assessed on all 4 language skills: Listening, Speaking, Reading and Writing. You will sit an exam for each of these skills in May or June of Year 11, but for your Writing test, you will do either a written exam in June of Year 11 or do written coursework during Years 10 and 11 of your French course. (For AQA modular French, see the section below.)

Your Speaking test will usually be carried out with your French teacher in April/May of Year 11. Each of the 4 exams in the skills counts for 25% of your total mark so each skill is equally important!

Which Tier will I take?

Each of the 4 skills has 2 levels or tiers: Foundation or Higher. This gives you 3 options. You will decide with your teacher which option is best for you.

Option 1 You take exams in all 4 language skills at the Foundation Tier (possible target grades G–C).

Option 2 You take exams in all 4 language skills at the Higher Tier (possible target grades D–A*)

Option 3 You 'mix and match'. This is a mixture of tiers for different exams (e.g. Speaking and Reading Higher, Listening and Writing Foundation) – according to your strengths and weaknesses. You teacher will be able to advise you on a final choice, probably in January/February.

If you attempt only Foundation Tier Papers your highest possible grade will be C. You can only reach Grade B or higher if you do mainly Higher Tier Papers.

If you do a written coursework option your teacher will give you tasks suitable for your level of ability – these may work out to give you enough marks to, for a Foundation Tier mark (maximum grade C) or a Higher Tier mark (maximum grade A*) for the written part of the exam.

Once your papers have been marked, a final mark for each of the 4 skills will be worked out for each paper by the Awarding Body. These marks will in turn be added up to give an overall total grade.

It is important to remember that your teacher is the best person to advise you on which tier to take for each language skill. It is also important that you know which tier you are doing for which skill before you start revising and before you take your exam as it will help you to focus your revision. Remember to check your exam paper on the day so that you know you are doing the correct one! You are only allowed to do one tier for each language skill involved.

Coursework option

All exam awarding bodies offer a coursework option as an alternative to one final written exam in Year 11. You will build up a file of written work during years 10 and 11 and usually 3 pieces of work are submitted to the awarding bodies. (NB 5 pieces for WJEC.) Your teacher will then choose the 3 (or 5) pieces of work which cover a variety of topics (called contexts or themes) and which show how well you can write in, for example, different tenses and different styles (eg letters, articles). The length of all 3 pieces together will be about 300 words for work to be considered for a Foundation grade (maximum C) and about 500 words for a Higher grade (maximum A*).

It is, however, very important to realise that if you want to get a grade C or above you must be able to use past, present and future tenses and to express personal opinions. It is a wise thing to try to produce at least 2 of these tenses in each piece of coursework. If you are aiming for an even higher grade you will have to work hard at producing not just different tenses but longer sentences which explain your opinions and link your ideas together.

Coursework done in controlled conditions

For WJEC – all 5 pieces of work must be completed in class, under the supervision of a teacher with no help from notes or reference materials. You may, however, use a dictionary.

For all awarding bodies, (AQA, EDEXCEL, OCR) candidates have to include at least one of their 3 pieces of work done under 'controlled conditions'. This, again, means that you can use a dictionary but no other notes, books or reference materials. You cannot ask anybody for help. Basically, it is like doing a piece of work in exam conditions, but in the classroom.

Coursework in non-controlled conditions (Independent coursework)

If you are doing non-controlled or independent coursework, your teacher will give you a title and allow you to do a first draft, probably at home. Check with your teacher and ask if you can make use of notes and exercise books (these are usually allowed for independent work), but avoid using text books – examiners can easily recognise chunks copied from text books – they want to see what you can produce! Your teacher is allowed to give you a checklist of things which you need to look at again, before your final draft. The final draft is the one which will be marked. Do not throw away your first draft or your checklist as these will need to be sent to the exam awarding bodies together with your final version.

There are lots of writing tasks in this book, together with tips of how to impress the examiners. So, work through the chapters in the order you meet the topics at school.

What happens with the AQA modular course – (Specification B)?

If you are following the AQA modular course, you will be assessed both during the course in Years 10 and 11 and at the end of your course in Year 11. You will work through the modules in this order.

Module 1 (My World, January of Year 10)

This module has tests at either Foundation or Higher for Listening and Reading. There is also a Speaking test with your teacher. You will study the following topics: Self, Family, Friends, Interests and Hobbies, Home and Local Environment, Daily Routine, School and Future Plans.

Module 2 (Holiday Time and Travel, June of Year 10)

This module has tests at either Foundation or Higher for Listening and Reading. You will study the following topics: Travel, Transport and Finding the Way, Tourism, Accommodation on Holiday Activities, Services.

Module 3 (Work and Lifestyle, Winter of Year 11)

This module is examined through coursework and candidates produce spoken and written work on the following topics: Home Life, Healthy Living, Part-Time Jobs and Work Experience, Leisure, Shopping.

Module 4 (The Young Person in Society – June Year 11)

This module has exams at Foundation or Higher in all 4 skills: Speaking, Listening, Reading, Writing. The exams cover new topics: Personal Relationships, The Environment, Education, Careers, Social Issues. The exams also cover topics studied in the first 3 modules.

If you study on this course, half of the marks for the whole of the course are examined in this last set of exams on Module 4.

During the exam

- Structure your time so that you have enough time to answer all of the questions. Don't spend too long on one question. First answer the questions you can do easily and then go back to the more difficult ones.
- Answer all the questions – make an intelligent guess if you are really stuck.
- Look carefully at the number of marks you can get for each question. For example, 3 marks means you must give 3 items of information on each answer.
- Stick to the point. Give opinions and reasons wherever you can and in your own written French use the different tenses where appropriate.
- Plan your answers, especially for the writing paper.
- Write clearly in blue or black ink. Remember to cross out neatly any work you don't want the examiner to mark.
- Leave some time at the end to look over your answers.
- Remember to answer in the correct language. On Reading and Listening papers, if the question is written in English, answer in English. If the question is in French, answer in French. Answers written in the wrong language will be ignored by the examiner.
- Learn the following instructions. If you do not understand the instructions you will not do yourself justice.

Most of the instructions on your exam papers will be in French. Some exam awarding bodies use the 'vous' form, e.g. complétez, others use the 'tu' form, e.g. complète. Make sure you know the following:

Arrange / Arrangez	= Arrange
... les mots dans le bon ordre	= ... the words in the right order
Choisis / Choisissez	= Choose
... les bonnes phrases, la bonne lettre	= ... the right sentences, the right letter
Coche / Cochez	= Tick
... la case appropriée, la bonne case	= ... the right box
Complète / Complétez	= Complete
... les détails, la grille	= ... the details, the grid
Copie / Copiez ...	= Copy ...
Corrige / Corrigez	= Correct
... les détails, les fautes, les erreurs	= ... the details, the mistakes
Décris / Décrivez ...	= Describe ...
Demande / Demandez	= Ask
... pourquoi	= ... why
Dessine / Dessinez	= Draw
... une flèche	= ... an arrow
Dis / Dites ...	= Say ...
Donne / Donnez les détails.	= Give the details.
En chiffres	= In figures
Ecris / Ecrivez	= Write
... le mot qui ne va pas avec les autres	= ... the word which doesn't go with the others
... les numéros, les lettres	= ... the numbers, the letters
... qui correspondent	= ... which match
... une carte, une lettre, en français	= ... a card, a letter, in French
Encercle / Encerclez oui ou non.	= Circle (draw a circle round) yes or no.
Explique / Expliquez	= Explain
... pourquoi, comment	= ... why, how

Fais / Faites une liste.	= Make a list.
Finis / Finissez	= Finish
Imagine / Imaginez	= Imagine
Indique / Indiquez	= Indicate
Lis / Lisez	= Read
... le texte, l'article	= ... the text, the article
Mets / Mettez	= Put
... les dessins dans le bon ordre	... the drawings in the right order
Note / Notez	= Note down
... les détails qui manquent	= ... the missing details
Où est / sont ...?	= Where is / are ...?
ou	= or
Pose / Posez des questions	= Ask questions
Prépare / Préparez	= Prepare
... un dépliant	= ... a leaflet
Quand?	= When?
Que veut dire ...?	= What does ... mean?
Quel problème?	= Which problem?
Quelle erreur?	= Which mistake?
Qui ...?	= Who ...?
Regarde / Regardez l'image.	= Look at the picture.
Remercie / Remerciez ...	= Thank ...
Remplis / Remplissez	= Fill in
... la grille, le formulaire	= ... the grid, the form
Réponds / Répondez aux questions en français.	= Answer the questions in French.
Tourne / Tournez la page.	= Turn the page.
Trouve / Trouvez	= Find
... l'erreur, la bonne réponse	= ... the mistake, the correct answer
Utilise / Utilisez les symboles.	= Use the symbols.
Vous n'aurez pas besoin de toutes les lettres.	= You will not need all the letters.
Vrai ou faux?	= True or false?

Last minute tips!

If you write in the wrong language you will not get any marks. For Reading and Listening exams, up to one-fifth of the marks may be awarded to questions which have English instructions or require answers written in English. Remember, if the instructions are in English you have to write out an answer in English. If the instructions are in French you have to write out an answer in French.

Listening

- Whichever awarding body you are taking, you will have 5 minutes to read through the paper before the exam starts. Use this time carefully – it will give you important clues about what you will be hearing and will reduce your 'panic factor'!
- Remember that you don't need to write in full sentences.
- Look carefully at the pictures in the questions.
- If you miss a question, don't panic, keep listening, you can have another 'go' in the second listen through!
- Write in the correct language!
- Don't agonise over a spelling; *provided your message is clear* examiners will tolerate mistakes!

Speaking

- Don't panic! Your teacher is there to help and is probably as nervous as you are about performing well!
- Remember your cue card if you are doing a presentation and arrive five minutes early.
- Read the English settings – they are there to explain the situation, put you at ease and to help!
- Try to spot the 'unexpected element' in the second Foundation, or the first Higher role play.
- While preparing, think what the examiner's lead-in question might be if you have a cue which says Répondez à la question, or reply to a question and how you could answer.
- If you don't understand a question or want something repeated, say so – Je n'ai pas compris la question. Répétez s'il vous plaît. This will give you a few seconds and keeps the French flowing!
- Remember: to get a C grade you need to use past, present and future tenses. Learn a few phrases in each of these tenses very thoroughly on each topic.
- Smile as you go in, it will relax you!

- Remember to work out exactly where you went on holiday last year, what you did last weekend, last night, this morning (perfect tense) and what you will do tonight, this weekend, in the summer, next year (future tense). Try not to fish around for ideas in the exam room – have your ideas 'straight' before you go in so that you only have to recall the appropriate phrases in French.

Reading

- Read through the text and questions once before you even attempt to answer any questions.
- Check that you understand the instructions.
- Examiners are checking that you have understood. Examiners will not deduct marks for incorrect spellings. But your message should be clear to gain marks.
- Try not to leave gaps – make an intelligent guess rather than leave a gap! You do not have to write in full sentences but, again, the message should be clear.

Writing

- Read the question at least twice before you start.
- Check the instructions.
- Plan your answer. It's easier if you think of four points, and write just a few sentences for each.
- On longer answers, examiners will look for accurate French, so check spellings and tenses very carefully.
- Do not 'experiment with new phrases' – stick to what you know and can say well.
- Remember to get those opinions in on longer letters and accounts.

If your exam is tomorrow, take a break and have a long bath! You could flick through the word lists (pages 79–108) for 20 minutes and then have a rest. Let your mind relax before the big day!

Bon courage!

Caroline Woods

Checklist

How do you feel about these?
In French, can you:

		Fine	Help!
1	say and spell your name?	☑	☐
2	give your nationality?	☑	☐
3	give your age and birthday?	☑	☐
4	describe yourself (physical appearance and character)?	☑	☑
5	give the same details about your family?	☑	☑
6	talk about your pets (size and colour)?	☑	☐
7	say where you live and spell it out?	☑	☐
8	say how you feel (ill, well, tired, hungry, thirsty, hot, cold, better)?	☐	☑
9	say where you have a pain?	☐	☑
10	ask for items at a chemist's?	☐	☑
11	call for help?	☐	☑

It's all about yourself!

Match up the checklist items with the Notes/Options below. Concentrate on the questions that you are less confident about and where you need some help. On pages 79–81 you will find vocabulary which will help you with this topic.

Help is at hand!

		Notes/Options
1	Comment tu t'appelles? Je m'appelle ...	
2	Tu es de quelle nationalité? Je suis anglais(e).	écossais(e), irlandais(e), gallois(e) *– For girls add an 'e'!*
3	Tu as quel âge? J'ai 16 ans.	*16 = seize not six!*
	Quelle est la date de ton anniversaire? C'est le 12 février.	*Make sure you know the months.*
4	Décris-toi s'il te plaît. Je suis assez grand(e) et de taille moyenne.	assez = quite petit(e) = small de taille moyenne = of medium build
	J'ai les cheveux blonds et courts.	courts = short
	Je suis timide, sympa et modeste!	timide = shy sympa = nice
5	Tu as des frères ou des soeurs? Non, je suis enfant unique.	= No, I'm an only child.
	Oui, j'ai une soeur et un frère. demi-frère demi-soeur	 = step-brother = step-sister
	Ma soeur s'appelle Catherine. Elle est amusante*, mince et intelligente*.	*– Adjectives marked * end in 'e' to describe a girl.*
	Mon frère s'appelle Paul. Il est amusant, et assez grand mais il est egoïste.	egoïste = selfish
	Paul a 12 ans. Catherine a 14 ans.	*Not* Paul *est* 12 ans!
	Décris ton père / ta mère. Ma mère s'appelle Anne. Elle est gentille. Elle a 40 ans.	gentille = nice
	Mon père s'appelle Mike. Il est calme. Il a 42 ans.	calme = easy going

To help you describe your family, look at the word list on page 79. Remember to revise numbers 1–100, and make sure you know all the ages of your family! Write the names of each member of your family next to each appropriate French word.

6	Tu as un animal domestique? Non je n'ai pas d'animal. Je n'ai pas de / d' ...	 = I haven't got ...
	Oui j'ai un chat / chien, etc. Il s'appelle Snowy – il est blanc et il a deux ans.	

The word list on page 79 has been designed to help you revise animals.

7	Où habites-tu? J'habite 24 Baker Road.	
	Ça s'écrit comment?	= How do you write it?
	Ça s'écrit B-A-K-E-R R-O-A-D.	

Listen to the alphabet on the CD (Chapter 1). Then check that you can spell out your name and address. You could also practise spelling the names of people in your family.

You'll soon need to make sure you know the colours. Check the words on page 79.

How's your memory?

AGE + EYES + HAIR	
J'ai	16 ans
Il a / Elle a	les yeux bleus les cheveux longs

SIZE + PERSONALITY	
Je suis	grand(e) / petit(e)*
Il est	intelligent
Elle est	amusante
** For girls add an 'e'!*	

Going for a C?

Expand your descriptions with basic opinions and give simple reasons for your views. You could use, for example:

J'aime ♥	Je n'aime pas X
J'adore ♥♥	Je déteste X X

You could also learn and use describing details such as **sympa** or **méchant** so that you can say why you like or dislike something or someone.

8 Comment vas-tu?	= How are you?
Je suis malade / fatigué(e).	= I'm ill / tired.
Ça ne va pas du tout.	= I'm not at all well.
J'ai faim / soif.	= I'm hungry / thirsty.
J'ai chaud / froid.	= I'm hot / cold.
9 Où as-tu mal?	= Where does it hurt?
J'ai mal à ...	*+ part of body*

Look at the word list on page 80 to help you feel more confident about saying which parts of the body are sore or feeling ill. Try to relate the vocabulary to your own body so that you know what you're talking about!

10 A la pharmacie	= At the chemist's

Use the word list on page 81 to memorise the important vocabulary here. Always try to picture what you're asking for: for example a tube of toothpaste and a bottle of aspirin.

11 Au secours!	= Help!

Take a break

Now try the Test yourself exercises! When you've done them, look back at the Checklist on page 7 – you should now feel fine about all the questions.

Test yourself

Task 1 **Listening**

Record the checklist questions and play back the cassette stopping after each question to give the answer. See how long you can talk about your family without being interrupted. Can you manage a minute? Well done! Practise the questions and answers with a friend.

Task 2 **Writing**

Ecrivez une lettre (60–80 mots) à un(e) correspondant(e) sur votre famille.

Task 3 **Listening**

Listen to the CD (Chapter 1) and have a go at this exercise. Remplissez les détails en français. Ecoutez deux fois.

Christophe

Age?................. 1 ans

Date d'anniversaire?........................ 2

Mère – âge?...................... 3 ans

Père – âge?....................... 4 ans

Soeurs/frères? combien?..................... 5

Animal?.................... 6 +...................... 7

Nom du village 8

Check your answers. More than five? Well done!

Task 4 **Writing**

Have a quick look at the Checklist again, then write out as much as you can without looking things up. When you've finished ask a friend to read it – pick someone who is also learning French. Can they understand it? Give yourself a point for each bit of information they can understand (for example: J'ai un frère = one point). More than six? Excellent!

Do you remember these?

Start off	Cher + boy's name Chère + girl's name
Finish off	A bientôt Amitiés Amicalement

Answers

TASK 3

1 16; **2** 22 septembre; **3** 43; **4** 41; **5** une soeur; **6** un lapin, **7** un chat; **8** MURVIEL.

Checklist

How do you feel about these?
In French, can you:

		Fine	Help!
1	do the Foundation Checklist on page 7?	☑	☑
2	describe your friends (how they look, character)?	☑	❑
3	say how you feel about your family and friends?	☑	❑
4	make arrangements to see a doctor / dentist?	❑	❑
5	ask and answer questions about medical treatment?	❑	❑
6	give details about your lifestyle (healthy / unhealthy)?	❑	❑

It's all about yourself!

Match up the Checklist items with the Notes/Options below. Concentrate on the questions that you are less confident about and where you need some help. Look at the word lists on pages 79–81.

HELP IS AT HAND!

Notes/Options

1 Look back again at the Foundation Checklist. If you feel confident, carry on!

2 Décris ta meilleure copine.

Elle s'appelle Chloë. Elle a 16 ans. Elle est grande et mince. Elle a les cheveux blonds et les yeux bleus. Elle est drôle et sympa. — drôle = amusante

Décris ton meilleur copain.

Il s'appelle Alex. Il a 15 ans. Il a les yeux marron et les cheveux courts et noirs. — marron = brown *– No 's' is added.* courts = short

Quelquefois il est bête et il m'énerve mais d'habitude il me fait rire. — bête = stupid; = he annoys me; = he makes me laugh

3 Tu t'entends bien avec ton frère / père / copain? — = Do you get on well with ...?

Tu t'entends bien avec ta soeur / mère / copine?

Oui, je m'entends bien avec lui / avec elle. — avec lui = with him; avec elle = with her

Non, je ne m'entends pas bien avec lui / elle. — = No I don't get on well with him / her.

You could be creative and draw a family tree of your family. Check the word list on page 79 for words you need.

Reasons for liking ☺	Reasons for disliking ☹
je l'aime parce qu'...	je ne l'aime pas parce qu'...
il / elle est sympa	il / elle est bête
il / elle est amusant(e)	il / elle m'énerve
il / elle m'aide	il / elle est egoïste
il / elle me fait rire	il / elle prend mes affaires

4 Prendre un rendez-vous — = To make an appointment

Je peux voir le docteur / le dentiste? — = Can I see the doctor / dentist?

le docteur = } doctor
le médecin = }

C'est urgent.

Je voudrais un rendez-vous cet après-midi / demain matin. — = I'd like an appointment this afternoon / tomorrow morning.

Take a look at the medical instructions vocabulary on page 81, and learn the phrases – especially those that might be said to you when you're feeling unwell.

5 Qu'est-ce que je dois faire? — = What should I do?

Est-ce que je dois rester au lit? — = Should I stay in bed?

Je dois prendre des médicaments? — = Should I take some medicine?

Il faut une ordonnance? — = Do I need a prescription?

C'est grave? — = Is it serious?

Remember the word lists on page 81 with the answers to these questions, and on page 80 with words for where you feel the pain!

6 Tu as un régime équilibré? — = Do you have a balanced diet?

Oui, je mange bien – je mange de façon equilibrée, par exemple de la viande, des légumes, des fruits et des produits laitiers. — = dairy products

Je ne saute pas les repas.	= I don't skip meals.
Je ne mange pas trop de sucre.	trop de = too much
C'est bon / mauvais pour la santé.	= It's healthy / unhealthy.
Il ne faut pas ...	= You shouldn't ...
... fumer / boire de l'alcool / se droguer	= ... smoke / drink alcohol / take drugs
... parce que ça nuit à la santé.	= ... because it damages your health.

Going for an A?

Be prepared to give details about your lifestyle such as what you eat / don't eat and which sports you do (when and how often?). Be ready to give your opinion and give a reason.

Opinion 'starters'		
Je pense que		bête
Je crois que	+ c'est	dangereux
		bien

HOW'S YOUR MEMORY?

pourquoi? = why?

parce que = because

Test yourself

Task 1 **Listening**

Listen to the CD (Chapter 1) and answer the questions in English.

La santé

At school, for Technology, you are doing a project on health and healthy eating. You decide to interview your penfriend's father to find out if people in France are aware of the importance of healthy eating.

Listen to what he says and take notes in English.

1 How did he know he was unfit? (two details) [2 marks]

2 What made him do something about it? [1 mark]

3 How did he alter his diet? (two details) [2 marks]

4 What other action did he take? [1 mark]

5 What criticism does he make of technological progress? [1 mark]

6 What example does he give of the way motorcars have changed people's habits for the worse? [1 mark]

Comment éviter le stress ...

un peu de travail

un peu de révision

une bonne alimentation

et un peu d'exercice

un peu de repos

+ 8 heures de sommeil

Task 2 **Speaking**

Here is some role play practice. You ring up to make an appointment at the doctor's. You feel tired and feverish and want to see him this evening.

1 Greet the receptionist and ask for an appointment.
2 Explain your symptoms.
3 Say when you want to see the doctor.
4 The doctor is not available at that time, what do you say?
5 Confirm the time (10:30) of the appointment.

Task 3 **Writing**

Ecrivez un article (100 mots) sur votre régime et votre santé. Etes-vous en forme?

(Before you tackle this writing exercise look back at the Checklist on page 7 and make sure you can answer the question as fully as possible.)

Remember to look back at the Checklist to see how much you've learned.

Answers

TASK 1

1 Always tired = 1 and couldn't climb stairs = 1
2 Saw picture of himself with daughter = 1
3 Started eating more fruit and vegetables = 1 and fewer cakes / pastries and fat / meat = 1
4 Joined a sports club / Did exercise = 1
5 Makes people lazy = 1
6 Used to go for a walk on Sunday = 1 but now go by car = 1

Total = 8

TASK 2

1 Bonjour Madame, je voudrais un rendez-vous avec le médecin / docteur.
2 Je suis fatigué et j'ai de la fièvre.
3 Je peux voir le docteur ce soir?
4 C'est possible demain matin?
5 D'accord à 10h 30. Merci Madame.

TASK 3

Ask your teacher if he or she would mind looking at your work. Be enthusiastic! Ask if he or she could say if the work is inaccurate, and, if so, which areas need further revision (such as vocabulary, verbs).

Thank him or her!

Well done – you've finished the chapter!

For your own notes

....

....

....

....

....

....

....

Chez moi – Foundation

Checklist

How do you feel about these?
In French, can you:

	Fine	Help!
1 give your address?	❑	❑
2 say whether you live in a house or a flat?	❑	❑
3 describe your house / flat, and say where it is?	❑	❑
4 name the rooms, and say how many there are?	❑	❑
5 find out about the rooms in somebody else's house?	❑	❑
6 describe your room (contents, colour, size) and say where it is?	❑	❑
7 give a description of the rooms, and say what you do in each room?	❑	❑
8 say if you have a garden and, if so, describe it?	❑	❑
9 give information about or ask about having a bath or a shower?	❑	❑
10 give information and find out about eating and other household routines?	❑	❑
11 say what jobs you do around the house?	❑	❑

Around the house

Use the word lists on pages 82–84 to make a spider diagram with the rooms in your house along with their contents and the things you do in each room. Remember that the more creative you are in your learning the more you'll know on the day of the exam. The more confident you are, the better your results!

Help is at hand!

	Notes/Options
1 Où habites-tu?	
J'habite (à) Southport.	
C'est une ville près de Liverpool.	une ville = a town près de = near
Où est Southport?	
C'est dans le nord-ouest de l'Angleterre.	le sud = south l'est = east le nord = north l'ouest = west
Quel est ton adresse? C'est ...	*– Be prepared to spell the road name.*
2 Tu habites une maison ou un appartement? J'habite une maison.	
3 Où se trouve ta maison? C'est en ville.	
dans la banlieue	= in the suburbs
à la campagne	= in the countryside
Comment est ta maison?	Comment est ...? = What is ... like?
Ma maison est grande.	
petite	= small
assez	= quite
assez grande	= quite big
C'est une maison mitoyenne	= semi detached
C'est une maison individuelle.	= detached

Look at the word list on page 84.

Comment est ton appartement? Mon appartement est grand – c'est dans	
un immeuble	= block of flats
au deuxième étage	= on the second floor
au premier étage	= on the first floor
4/5	
Combien de pièces y a-t-il?	
Il y a huit pièces – le salon, la salle à manger, le bureau,	Il y a = There is / are le bureau = the study
trois chambres et la salle de bains. Il y a aussi une cave.	une cave = a cellar
6 Qu'est-ce qu'il y a dans ta chambre? Il y a un lit, une commode, une armoire, une chaise, une table et une télévision.	

Revise colours! Draw and label a blob with each of the colours on page 79.

De quelle couleur est ta chambre? Ma chambre est blanche, la moquette est bleue et les rideaux sont bleus.	 = the carpet = the curtains
Où est ta chambre? Elle est / C'est au premier étage, à côté de la salle de bains.	 à côté de = next to en face de = opposite
7 Comment sont les pièces chez toi?	= What are the rooms at your house like?

Use the word lists on pages 82–83 to help you describe the different rooms in your house.

Que fais-tu dans ta chambre / la salle à manger? Qu'est-ce qu'on fait dans le salon? On regarde la télévision. On écoute des CD.	Que fais-tu? = What do you do? *– If you hear* **on** *in a question, e.g. Qu'est-ce qu'on fait ... ? you will need to use* **on** *in the answer.*

The word lists on pages 83–84 helps you say what you do in the different rooms of your house. If you need other words or phrases, check in the dictionary, or ask a friend or your teacher. Learn at least three activities by heart.

8 Est-ce qu'il y a un jardin chez toi? Oui, il y a un grand jardin.	
Comment est ton jardin? Il y a des fleurs, des arbres et une pelouse.	des fleurs = some flowers des arbres = some trees une pelouse = a lawn

Mental block with garden words? Write the words on page 85 – within the outline of a wheelbarrow!

9 Est-ce que je peux ... ?	= Can I ... ?
... prendre un bain?  ... prendre une douche?	*– Remember to say please!* **S'il te plaît** *to a friend, but* **s'il vous plaît** *to an adult, such as a penfriend's parent.*
Où est la salle de bains?	= Where is the bathroom?
Je peux avoir une serviette s'il vous plaît?	= Please can I have a towel?
Je peux avoir du savon s'il vous plaît?	= Please can I have some soap?
La douche ne marche pas! 	= The shower isn't working! le robinet = the tap

Revise telling the time (page 113) to be able to say at what time you do certain things.

10 A quelle heure est-ce que tu prends ton petit déjeuner? Je prends le petit déjeuner à huit heures.	le petit déjeuner = breakfast le déjeuner = lunch le dîner = evening meal
A quelle heure est-ce que tu quittes la maison le matin? Je quitte la maison à huit heures et demie.	le matin = in the morning
A quelle heure est-ce que tu te lèves? Je me lève à sept heures.	= What time do you get up?
A quelle heure est-ce que tu te couches? Je me couche à 10 heures et demie.	= What time do you go to bed?
11 Que fais-tu pour aider chez toi? Je fais la vaisselle, je range ma chambre et je lave la voiture.	= What do you do to help at home? = I do the washing up je range = I tidy up = I wash the car

For your own notes

....

....

....

....

....

....

....

....

Going for a C?

Time markers	
d'habitude	= normally
quelquefois	= sometimes
souvent	= often
puis	= then
ensuite	= next
après	= afterwards
tous les jours	= every day
toujours	= always

Give as many details as possible, say *when*, *where* and *how often* things happen at home.

Give simple opinions such as **J'aime / Je n'aime pas**.

Use the perfect tense (see pages 109 and 128) to talk about what you did last night and the future tense (see pages 112 and 130) to talk about what you will do at home tonight / next weekend / tomorrow.

In the role play exercises, be prepared to listen to the teacher – you will have one task starting: **répondez à la question** ... As you prepare your role play, try to think ahead to what the question might be.

– Use a selection of the time markers listed above.

Test yourself

Task 1 **Speaking**

Record the Checklist questions and then answer them all in French without looking at the notes. You might need a few attempts before getting them all right.

Now try to talk for a minute about your room (size, contents, colour) – whenever you get a bit stuck, look at the word lists on pages 82–83 to help.

Task 2 **Speaking**

Here's a role play exercise: you arrive at a French friend's house and you want to have a shower.

1 Ask where the bathroom is.

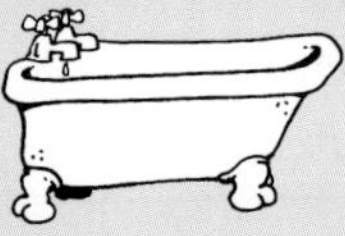

'où'

2 Say you would like to have a shower.

3 Ask for a towel.

4 Ask for some soap.

Task 3 **Writing**

Write to a friend, using 60–80 words, about your home and daily routines. Refer back to the Notes/Options if you need some help. Remember to use **Cher** or **Chère** to start, and **Amitiés** or **Amicalement** to finish.

When you've written the letter, ask a friend who is also learning French to read it. Give yourself a point for each detail they understand.

More than eight points? Brilliant!

Task 4 **Writing**

Draw a flow chart about what you did at home last night. Start by using **Hier soir** ...

The following structures might be helpful:

j'ai mangé	= I ate
j'ai bu	= I drank
j'ai lu	= I read
j'ai pris	= I took
je suis allé(e)*	= I went
je me suis couché(e)*	= I went to bed
j'ai regardé	= I watched
j'ai aidé	= I helped
j'ai travaillé	= I worked
j'ai fait	= I did / made
je suis arrivé(e)*	= I arrived

– Note: girls add the extra 'e'.

Answers

TASK 2

1 Où est la salle de bains? **2** Je peux prendre une douche? **3** Je peux avoir une serviette s'il te plaît? **4** Je voudrais du savon s'il te plaît.

Checklist

How do you feel about these?
In French, can you:

		Fine	Help!
1	answer the questions on the Foundation Checklist on page 12?	❑	❑

If you've ticked the Help! box, go back to the Foundation Notes/Options and revise!

		Fine	Help!
2	discuss and express opinions about meals, meal times and eating habits?	❑	❑
3	talk about your daily routines in the past and future?	❑	❑
4	say you'll help out, or ask for help around the house?	❑	❑
5	say how you share jobs at home?	❑	❑
6	say if you share a room?	❑	❑

Around the house

Draw the outline of a house divided into rooms. Label each room. Then write a sentence for each room, e.g. contents, what you do there (the word lists on pages 82–84 will help you!). Remember that the more creative you are in your learning the more you'll know on the day of the exam. The more confident you are, the better your results!

HELP IS AT HAND!

Notes/Options

1 Once you've looked back at the Foundation Checklist and feel confident, carry on!

2 Quel est ton plat préféré?

= What's your favourite dish?

Mon plat préféré est ...

– Look ahead to Chapter 8 to talk about food and drink.

Qu'est-ce que tu préfères boire?
Je préfère boire ...
Ma boisson préférée est ...

A quelle heure préfères-tu manger le soir?
Je préfère manger à sept heures.

Qu'est-ce que tu n'aimes pas manger?
Je n'aime pas / Je déteste manger ...

– It's a good idea, and much more interesting, to talk about the things you really like eating, although you need to know how to say what you don't like as well.

POSITIVE	NEGATIVE
J'adore la moutarde. Je préfère ... J'aime beaucoup ... C'est délicieux ... C'est super. C'est savoureux (tasty). Ça sent bon. (It smells good.) C'est bon pour la santé.	Je deteste la moutarde. Je n'aime pas ... Je ne mange pas de viande. Je ne bois pas de vin. C'est trop sucré / salé. (It's too sweet / salty.) Ça me donne mal au coeur. (It makes me feel sick.) Je n'aime pas le goût. C'est mauvais pour la santé.

– To talk about what you did last night, hier soir, *or this morning,* ce matin, *you need to put verbs into the perfect tense (e.g. ate, drank). (Word list page 109.)*

3 Qu'est-ce que tu as fait ce matin?

= What did you do this morning?

Ce matin je **me suis réveillé(e)** à sept heures.

Puis, je **me suis lavé(e)** et je **me suis habillé(e)**.

Après, je **suis descendu(e)** dans la cuisine où **j'ai pris** mon petit déjeuner. **J'ai mangé** des céréales et j'ai bu du thé. **J'ai quitté** la maison à huit heures.

– See page 128 for a revision of the perfect tense.

– To talk about what you will do tonight, ce soir, *tomorrow,* demain, *or next week,* la semaine prochaine, *put the verbs into the future tense (e.g. will eat, will drink). See the word list on page 112.*

Que feras-tu demain soir?

= What will you do tomorrow evening?

– See page 130 for a revision of the future tense.

Demain soir j'**arriverai** chez moi à cinq heures. Je **regarderai** la télévision puis je **prendrai** le dîner. Après je **ferai** la vaisselle et je **ferai** mes devoirs. A neuf heures je **regarderai** la télévision ou **j'écouterai** mes disques. Puis à dix heures je **prendrai** une douche et je me **coucherai**.

– *Listen for the time markers such as* hier *or* demain *and use the appropriate tense!*

4 Je peux t'aider?	= Can I help you? (to a friend)
Je peux te donner un coup de main?	
Je peux vous aider?	= Can I help you? (to an older person)
Je peux aider à faire la vaisselle?	= Can I help do the washing up?

Draw a mini-picture and label each chore listen on page 82. You will need to be able to talk about all the rotten chores – even if you never do them!

5 Qu'est-ce que tu dois faire chez toi?	= What do you have to do at home?
Je dois ranger ma chambre.	= I have to tidy my room.
Et les autres?	= And the others?
Ma soeur doit faire la vaisselle tous les jours.	*– Add extra detail such as* **tous les jours / deux fois par semaine** *wherever you can.*
Ce n'est pas juste!	= It's not fair!
C'est trop!	= It's too much!
Ce n'est pas assez!	= It's not enough!
Je fais plus / que lui / qu'elle!	= I do more than him/ her!
A mon avis, il / elle est paresseux / paresseuse.	= In my opinion, he / she is lazy.
Il devrait faire la vaisselle plus souvent.	= He ought to wash up more often.

6 Tu partages ta chambre?	= Do you share your bedroom?
Oui, je partage ma chambre avec ma soeur.	
Non, j'ai une chambre à moi.	
Non, j'ai ma propre chambre.	propre *before the noun* = **own**
J'ai une chambre propre.	propre *after the noun* = **clean**

Going for an A?

Revise the conditional tense (see page 131) then try the Test yourself tasks. The writing activity practises the use of the conditional tense. Remember that the examiners reward tenses other than the present, perfect and future as well as expressions such as the ones in the Checklist. Don't forget to learn the parts of the verbs in the conditional tense which allow you to describe the actions of other people, for example: il / elle voudrait, ils / elles aimeraient.

Try to talk for a minute about how you help out at home. For example, say which jobs you do and how you feel about doing them; which rooms you do each job in and at what time of day. When you know what you're going to say, set about recording yourself and then play it back to check how you sound.

If you get stuck for things to say, remember that you can comment on what people do **not** do. For example:

Mon frère **ne** fait **pas** la vaisselle – ce **n'**est **pas** juste.

Test yourself

Task 1 **Writing**

Write between 100 – 120 words on
Ma chambre idéale.

j'aimerais = I would like	j'aimerais acheter = I would like to buy
je voudrais = I would like	il y aurait = there would be
j'aimerais avoir = I would like to have	

Add why you would like to have or buy something, and use lots of adjectives about colour, size, etc.
When you've written it, ask your teacher to check your work for accuracy. Remember to thank him / her!

Task 2 **Listening**

Have a go at this CD exercise (Chapter 2). Play it twice.

Les tâches ménagères
Ecoutez les trois jeunes.
Cochez la case Vrai ou la case Faux.

	Vrai	**Faux**
Exemple Pierre doit ranger sa chambre.	☑	❑
Pierre		
1 Pierre fait la cuisine souvent.	❑	❑
2 Pierre pense que son frère aide moins que lui.	❑	❑
3 Il trouve la situation injuste.	❑	❑
Christelle		
4 Le week-end Christelle fait la vaisselle.	❑	❑
5 Christelle déteste cuisiner.	❑	❑
Paul		
6 Normalement, Paul doit débarrasser la table.	❑	❑
7 Paul s'énerve parce qu'il pense qu'il aide assez.	❑	❑

Remember to look back at the Checklist.

Answers

TASK 2
1 Faux **2** Vrai **3** Vrai **4** Faux **5** Faux
6 Faux **7** Vrai

Well done – you've finished the chapter!

For your own notes

....

....

....

....

....

....

....

....

....

....

....

....

....

....

....

....

Mes passe-temps – Foundation

Checklist

How do you feel about these?
In French, can you:

		Fine	Help!
1	understand and give details about your interests and how you spend your free time (hobbies, sports, clubs, music)?	❑	❑
2	say how long you have had your interests?	❑	❑
3	give simple opinions about your activities, and say why you like or dislike doing certain things?	❑	❑
4	ask what a friend does?	❑	❑
5	ask what a friend would like to do?	❑	❑
6	ask for and give information about when activities start and finish?	❑	❑
7	arrange to meet at a certain time and place?	❑	❑
8	buy tickets for pool, sports ground, leisure activities?	❑	❑
9	apologise for being late?	❑	❑
10	say what kind of films and TV programmes you watch?	❑	❑
11	say how you spend your pocket money?	❑	❑
12	say what there is to do in the area where you live?	❑	❑
13	say what you did recently (such as last weekend)?	❑	❑
14	say what you plan to do (such as next weekend)?	❑	❑

Time out for leisure

This could be one of your favourite subjects, so make the most of it and enjoy using the vocabulary and phrases. Write a really really long sentence with at least five things you do! Link them with 'et' (and) or 'puis' (then). Look at pages 85–88 for help.

HELP IS AT HAND!

		Notes/Options
1	Qu'est-ce que tu fais pendant ton temps libre?	

Look up the activities on page 85 and visualise yourself doing each activity while saying the French expression. That way you're more likely to remember!

		Notes/Options
	Je fais du vélo, je sors avec mes amis.	
	Je joue au tennis et je nage.	
	jouer au foot	= to play football
	jouer au basket	= to play basketball
	Je lis, j'aime les livres de science-fiction et je lis des magazines.	je lis = je fais de la lecture
	Je joue du piano.	= I play the piano.
	Je joue de la guitare.	= I play the guitar.
	Je vais au cinéma / au club des jeunes.	
	Je fais partie d'un orchestre / d'un groupe.	= I'm a member of an orchestra / a group.
2	Depuis combien de temps est-ce que tu fais ça?	= How long have you been doing that?
	Depuis un an / depuis deux ans.	= For one / two years.
3	Ça te plaît la natation? Tu aimes la natation? Oui, j'aime beaucoup la natation.	= Do you like swimming? j'aime = I like j'adore = I really like
	Tu aimes jouer de la guitare? Oui, j'adore jouer de la guitare.	= Do you like playing the guitar?
	Pourquoi?	
	Je joue bien et j'aime la musique. C'est intéressant.	= I play well and I like music. It's interesting.
	Tu es sportif / sportive?	= Are you fond of sport? sportif = masculine sportive = feminine
	Non, je ne suis pas sportif / sportive.	
	Je n'aime pas le sport. Je ne joue pas bien et c'est fatigant.	fatigant = tiring
	Tu aimes la musique?	
	Oui, j'adore la musique pop.	

J'aime le rock. Mon groupe préféré s'appelle ...	= My favourite group is called ...
4 Que fais-tu pendant ton temps libre?	= What do you do in your free time?
5 Que veux-tu faire ce soir / samedi?	= What would you like to do this evening / on Saturday?

– *If you want to ask a friend if he or she would like to do a particular thing use* **tu veux** *+ infinitive.* *(See page 132.)*

Tu veux ...	= Do you want ...
... nager?	= ... to go swimming?
... sortir?	= ... to go out?
... jouer au tennis?	= ... to play tennis?

– *If you want to suggest going somewhere, you use:*

Tu veux aller + à la piscine?	= to the swimming pool?
Tu veux aller + au cinéma?	= to the cinema?
Si on allait + aux magasins?	= to the shops?
6 ... commence à quelle heure?	= When does the ... start?
le film	= film
la pièce	= play
le concert	= the concert
le match	= the match
La séance commence à huit heures du soir.	= The performance starts at 8 pm.
A quelle heure finit le film?	A quelle heure? = at what time?
Le film finit à dix heures du soir.	finit = finishes du soir = in the evening

– *Starting and finishing times might need the 24-hour clock; so remember 7 pm =* 19 heures.

7 On se rencontre à ...	= We'll meet at ...

Write invitations to three places in three big speech bubbles (see page 88 for help).

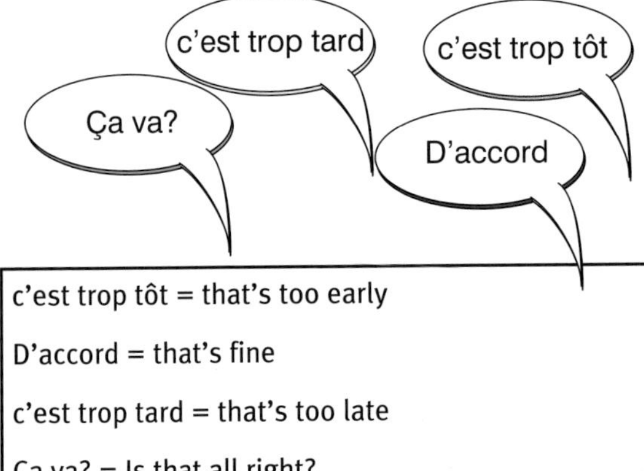

c'est trop tôt = that's too early
D'accord = that's fine
c'est trop tard = that's too late
Ça va? = Is that all right?

8 Je voudrais une place ...	une place = a seat
... au balcon	= in the balcony
... à l'orchestre	= in the stalls
Je voudrais un billet.	= I'd like a ticket.
9 Je suis désolé(e), je suis en retard!	= I'm sorry, I'm late!
10 Tu regardes souvent la télévision?	
Oui je regarde la télévision tous les soirs.	tous les soirs = every evening
Quelle sorte d'émissions préfères-tu?	
Je préfère ...	

Visualise programmes you know as you learn the different types of TV programmes and practise giving reasons why you like or dislike them! See page 87.

Tu vas souvent au cinéma?	
Je vais au cinéma une fois par mois.	une fois = once par mois = a month (per month / monthly)
Quelle sorte de films préfères-tu?	
11 On te donne de l'argent de poche?	= Do you get pocket money?
Je reçois 10 euros par mois / par semaine.	= I get 10 euros a month / a week.
Non, je gagne de l'argent.	= No, I earn money.
Est-ce que tu dépenses ton argent de poche?	tu dépenses = you spend
Oui, j'achète des magazines et des vêtements.	= Yes, I buy magazines and clothes.
12 Qu'est-ce qu'il y a à faire pour les jeunes dans ta ville?	= What is there for young people to do in your town?
Il y a un cinéma, un centre de loisirs, une piscine et une discothèque.	
On peut aller au cinéma, faire du sport, nager et aller à la discothèque.	– **On peut** *+ infinitive = one can / you can + activity*

13 Qu'est-ce que tu as fait le week-end dernier?

Activities (perfect tense)
j'ai joué = I played
j'ai vu un film = I saw a film
je suis allé(e) = I went
je suis sorti(e) = I went out
j'ai fait du vélo = I went on a bike ride
je me suis bien amusé(e) = I enjoyed myself

Revise the perfect tense (pages 128–129) so that you can talk about what you did in the past, such as last weekend. See page 86.

Time markers – use perfect tense	
samedi dernier	= last Saturday
hier soir	= last night
la semaine dernière	= last week

More time markers – use future tense	
ce soir	= this evening
demain (soir)	= tomorrow (evening)
samedi prochain	= next Saturday
ce week-end	= this weekend
le week-end prochain	= next weekend

14 Qu'est-ce que tu vas faire ce week-end?

Remember the two ways to talk about future plans?

A Use **je vais** + infinitive.

Je vais sortir. = I am going to go out.
Je vais aller au cinéma. = I am going to go to the cinema.
Je vais jouer au tennis. = I am going to play tennis.

B Use the future tense (see pages 112 and 130).

Activities (future tense)
je jouerai = I will play
je verrai = I will see
j'irai = I will go
je sortirai = I will go out
je ferai du vélo = I will go on a bike ride
je m'amuserai = I will have a good time

Going for a C?

'Pad out' your descriptions of the activities you do. For example, say when and how often you do things. And remember to say why you like certain things. Have another look back at the Notes/Options 13 and 14.

Write to a French friend, Amina. Describe what you did last weekend (100 words).

Notice the time marker **dernier** – this points to the past! Remember to use the perfect tense.

- In your written work examiners will look for what you have to say (communication) as well as the way you say it (accuracy).
- Make sure you understand the question before you start. Vital words are the time markers as they give you clues about which time zone you are in and which tense you need (future, perfect or present).

Whilst revising, you can check spellings with dictionaries, but you may need further help from a teacher.

Look at this answer.

Gloucester
le 7 mai

Chère Amina,

J'espère que tu vas bien. J'ai passé un très bon week-end. Vendredi, je suis sortie avec mes amis. Je suis allée au cinéma et j'ai vu un film d'aventure. C'était chouette. Samedi je me suis levée à 11 heures. L'après-midi, j'ai nagé à la piscine et samedi soir je suis allée à une boum chez Paul. J'ai dansé et j'ai bavardé. Je me suis bien amusée.

Hier, j'ai fait du vélo à la campagne (c'était fatigant!) et hier soir j'ai écouté un nouveau CD puis j'ai regardé la télévision.

Ecris-moi vite!

Amitiés

Eli

Check through your answer and highlight all the verbs in the perfect tense. Then learn them all!

Remember only girls add the extra 'e': je suis sorti(e), je suis allé(e). (See page 129.)

Take a break

Now try the Test yourself exercises! When you've done them, look back at the Checklist on page 18 – you should now be feeling fine for all of the questions.

Test yourself

Task 1 **Reading**

Lisez les descriptions des passe-temps.

Marc

Je fais de la natation et je joue souvent au foot – j'adore ça. Je suis très sportif.

Anne

Moi, j'aime beaucoup la musique, j'adore écouter des CDs et je vais souvent au cinéma.

Julie

Je fais du cheval le samedi et le dimanche je sors – je fais du vélo avec mes amis. C'est génial.

Xavier

Le soir je joue avec mon ordinateur et je joue de la guitare – je fais partie d'un groupe. J'aime lire aussi.

Regardez les dessins:

a

b

c

d

e

f

g

h

i

j

Indiquez les passe-temps de Marc, Anne, Julie et Xavier.

Exemple: Marc a + g
Anne .... + ...
Julie .... + ...
Xavier .... + ... + ...

Task 2 **Speaking**

Go through the checklist and the Notes/ Options with a friend. See how long you can talk about your interests. Use written prompts such as **le soir**, **le week-end**, **le sport** to jog your memory.

Can you talk for one minute?

Task 3 **Writing**

Ecrivez une liste de vos passe-temps, 1–10.

Exemple 1. Je regarde la télévision. Try to write out ten things! Use the word lists on pages 85–88 to help you to check.

If you've got more than six things – that's great!

Task 4 **Writing**

Write a letter (60–80 words). Describe what you normally do at the weekends and in the evening.

Use the present tense and time markers such as **d'habitude** and **normalement**.

Ask a friend to read the letter and give you a point for everything he or she understands. For example: Je vais au cinéma = 1 point. You should aim for six points.

Answers

TASK 1

Anne i + j Julie h + d

Xavier e + b + c

Checklist

How do you feel about these?
In French, can you:

		Fine	Help!
1	answer the questions on the Foundation Checklist on page 18?	❑	❑

If you've ticked the Help! box, go back to the Foundation Notes/Options and revise!

		Fine	Help!
2	understand and give preferences and opinions about your hobbies and activities (and those of other people)?	❑	❑
3	discuss and give opinions about films and TV programmes?	❑	❑
4	say what you would like to do if you had the money and the time?	❑	❑

Time out for leisure

This could be one of your favourite subjects, so make the most of it and enjoy using the vocabulary and phrases. The word lists on pages 85–88 will help you learn all the material for giving opinions about a film, discussing sports and hobbies and the things you like most.

Help is at hand!

	Notes/Options
1 Having looked back at the Foundation Checklist, do you feel really confident? If so, then carry on!	
2 Quel est ton passe-temps préféré?	préféré = favourite
Je préfère jouer au tennis.	– *You need an infinitive after* je préfère.
Je préfère faire de la voile.	faire de la voile = sailing
Mon passe-temps préféré – c'est faire de la voile.	
3 Que penses-tu de ... ?	

See the word list on page 87 for phrases to give your opinion.

4 Que ferais-tu si tu avais beaucoup d'argent et beaucoup de temps libre?	
Si j'avais beaucoup d'argent et beaucoup de temps libre j'irais ...	= If I had lots of money and free time I would go ...

j'irais = I would go

j'achèterais = I would buy

je jouerais = I would play

je ferais beaucoup de sport = I would do a lot of sport

Going for an A?

Revise the conditional tense on page 131.

Be ready to give your opinion and say why you have that opinion!

The following opinions are mixed up! Make up two lists, one positive (**c'est cool!**) and one negative (**c'est moche!**) Use a dictionary to help if you get stuck.

1 ça élimine le stress
2 ça me change les idées
3 c'est ennuyeux
4 c'est une perte de temps
5 ce n'est pas cher
6 ça m'intéresse
7 c'est bête
8 c'est trop cher
9 c'est bon pour la santé
10 c'est sans intérêt
11 c'est bien de rester entre copains
12 ça (me) détend
13 ça me stresse
14 c'est génial
15 c'est reposant
16 ça prend trop de temps
17 c'est fatigant

Now say what you like / dislike doing (see the word list on page 85 for lots of ideas) and link it to a **cool** or **moche** expression! These might be useful:

j'adore faire du sport
ça me détend
ça élimine le stress
c'est bon pour la santé

Test yourself

Task 1 **Speaking**

Prepare a talk 1–2 minutes long.

Try to say at least two things on each point and remember to give preferences and reasons why. Use the following cues:

Mes activités
le soir / le week-end
quand? souvent?
avec qui? où?
préférences? pourquoi?

You'll also find the Plan below useful.

Task 2 **Listening**

This is a CD exercise (Chapter 3 Higher). Listen twice.

Cécile et Marc vont au cinéma.

Cochez la case Vrai ou la case Faux.

Example

	Vrai	Faux
Cécile is free tomorrow.	☑	❑

		Vrai	Faux
1	A romantic film is on at the Gaumont.	❑	❑
2	Cécile thinks this kind of film is interesting.	❑	❑
3	Marc suggests seeing a comedy.	❑	❑
4	Hélène saw the film last night.	❑	❑
5	Hélène thought the film was fascinating.	❑	❑
6	Marc suggests meeting at 7:30pm at the café.	❑	❑
7	Hélène asks Marc to walk her home after the film.	❑	❑

Task 3 **Writing**

Ecrivez un article (120 mots) sur les loisirs et les jeunes dans ta ville.

Answers

Going for an A?

C'est cool! = 1, 2, 5, 6, 9, 11, 12, 14, 15.
C'est moche! = 3, 4, 7, 8, 10, 13, 16, 17.

TASK 2

1 Vrai **2** Faux **3** Faux **4** Vrai **5** Vrai **6** Vrai **7** Faux

Plan

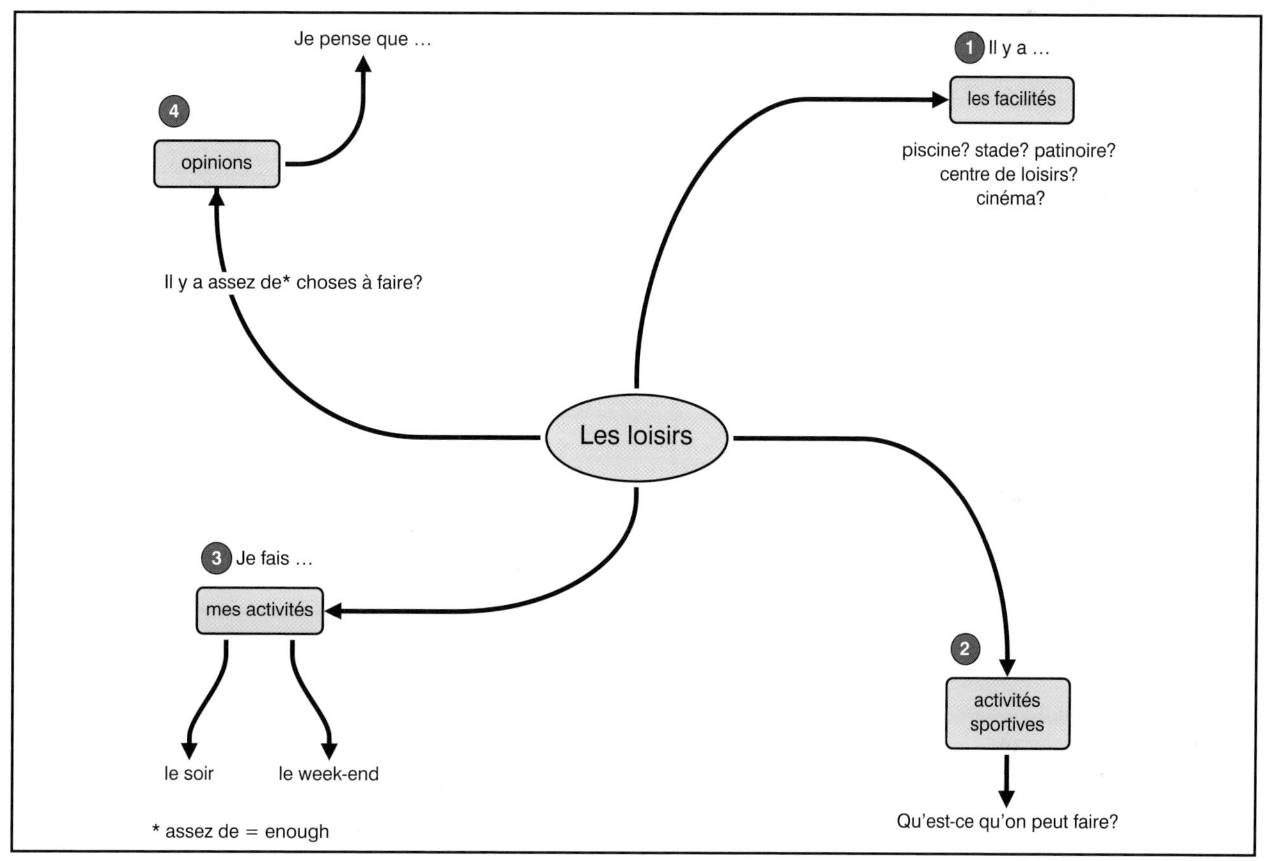

Checklist

How do you feel about these?
In French, can you:

	Fine	Help!
1 check in, say who you are and say a reservation has been made?	❑	❑
2 ask what rooms are available?	❑	❑
3 give details, such as kind of room, length of stay?	❑	❑
4 ask the cost?	❑	❑
5 ask to see the room?	❑	❑
6 ask about the facilities?	❑	❑
7 ask about keys and leaving / returning times to the hotel?	❑	❑
8 ask about meals (times, availability)?	❑	❑
9 say you want to pay the bill?	❑	❑
At a youth hostel		
10 ask to hire a sleeping bag?	❑	❑
11 understand hostel rules?	❑	❑
At a campsite		
12 ask for space for a tent or a caravan?	❑	❑
13 ask about facilities?	❑	❑
14 ask about rules?	❑	❑
General		
15 make a simple complaint (such as lack of hot water)?	❑	❑
16 write a booking letter and understand the reply?	❑	❑
17 ask for details about a town or region you want to visit?	❑	❑

Where are you staying?

Break any topic you revise into smaller, more manageable parts, e.g. think of 'hotel' as – 1. what kind of room? 2. what facilities in the hotel? 3. when things go wrong. Imagine actually arriving at a hotel: be creative and feel free to use language from other topics. Picturing the situation will help you remember the phrases better.

Help is at hand!

		Notes/Options
1	Bonjour Monsieur / Madame, je m'appelle ...	
	J'ai fait une réservation pour ma famille.	= I've made a reservation for my family.
	J'ai téléphoné pour réserver des chambres.	= I phoned to reserve rooms.
	J'ai écrit pour réserver des chambres.	= I wrote to reserve rooms.

You'll find the word list on page 89 useful at this stage.

2	Vous avez des chambres pour ce soir?	= Have you got any rooms for tonight?
	Vous avez de la place pour ce soir?	= Have you any space for tonight?
	Vous avez une chambre pour deux personnes?	= Have you got a double room?
	Vous avez une chambre pour une personne?	= Have you got a single room?
3	Je voudrais une chambre pour moi-même.	moi-même = myself
	Je voudrais une chambre pour mes parents / mes amis.	
	C'est pour une nuit.	= It's for one night.
	Je voudrais une chambre avec téléphone.	= I'd like a room with a phone.
	grand lit	= double bed
	douche	= shower
	salle de bains	= bathroom
	balcon	= balcony
	vue sur mer	= seaview
4	C'est combien une chambre?	= How much is a room?
	Ça fait combien par nuit?	par nuit = per night
	C'est trop cher!	= It's too expensive!
	Le petit déjeuner est compris?	= Is breakfast included?

5 Je peux voir la chambre s'il vous plaît?	= Can I see the room, please?

The word list on page 89 is useful for memorising the vocabulary at the hotel.

6 Est-ce qu'il y a un parking à l'hôtel?	= Is there a car park in the hotel?
un ascenseur	= a lift
Est-ce qu'il y a un téléphone dans la chambre?	= Is there a phone in the room?
un sèche-cheveux	= a hair-dryer
7 Je peux avoir la clé?	= Can I have the key?
C'est quelle chambre?	= Which room is it?
C'est la chambre 210 au deuxième étage.	= It's room 210 on the 2nd floor.
L'hôtel ferme à quelle heure?	= When does the hotel close?
Je peux avoir une clé pour la porte d'entrée?	= Can I have a front door key?
Vous tapez un code pour entrer.	= You have to key in a code to get in.
8 Le petit déjeuner est à quelle heure?	= What time is breakfast?
Je voudrais la demi-pension.	= I'd like half board.
On sert le dîner à partir de 19 heures jusqu'à 21 heures 30.	= Dinner is served from 7–9.30 pm.
9 Je voudrais payer s'il vous plaît.	= I'd like to pay please.
Je peux avoir la note s'il vous plaît?	= Please can I have the bill?
Vous acceptez les cartes de crédit?	= Do you accept credit cards?
10 Je peux louer un sac de couchage?	= Can I hire a sleeping bag?
une couverture	= a blanket
la salle à manger	= the dining room
le dortoir	= the dormitory
Où est le dortoir pour garçons / filles?	= Where is the boys'/ girls' dormitory?
Voici ma carte (de membre).	= Here is my (membership) card.
Où sont les lavabos?	= Where are the washbasins?
Où sont les WC?	= Where are the toilets?
Est-ce qu'il y a une tâche à faire?	= Is there a job to do?

See the word list on page 90 to check that you know the tasks you might be asked to do.

11 Vous êtes priés de ...	= You are requested to ...
Il est interdit (de manger dans le dortoir).	= It is forbidden (to eat in the dormitory). / No (eating in the dormitory).
La porte est fermée à 11 h du soir.	= The door is closed at 11 pm.
L'auberge ferme à 23 h.	= The hostel closes at 11 pm.
12 Au camping	= At the campsite
Je voudrais un emplacement pour une tente.	= I'd like a plot for a tent.
une caravane	= a caravan
Vous êtes combien?	= For how many people?
On est cinq, deux adultes et trois enfants.	= There are five of us, two adults and three children.
une place	= a plot
un emplacement	= a plot
à l'ombre	= in the shade
sous les arbres	= under the trees
loin de la discothèque	= a long way from the disco
près du lac	= near the lake
13 Est-ce qu'il y a une piscine?	= Is there a swimming-pool?
une alimentation	= a food shop
une boulangerie	= a baker's
14 Est-ce qu'on peut allumer un feu?	= Can I / we light a fire?

Est-ce qu'on peut faire un barbecue?	= Can I / we have a barbecue?
Est-ce que'il est interdit d'allumer un feu?	= Is it forbidden to light a fire?
Il faut laisser la voiture au parking après dix heures du soir.	= You have to leave the car in the car park after 10 pm.
Il est interdit de circuler après 22h.	= You must not drive around after 10 pm.

15 Problèmes! A l'hôtel.

Excusez-moi Monsieur / Madame mais ...

Il n'y a pas d'eau chaude.	= There isn't any hot water.
Il n'y a pas de serviette.	= There isn't a towel.
La télévision ne marche pas.	= The television doesn't work.
Le chauffage ne marche pas.	= The heating doesn't work.
La douche ne marche pas.	= The shower doesn't work.
Il y a beaucoup de bruit.	= There is a lot of noise.
La chambre n'est pas propre!	= The room isn't clean!

Going for a C?

Read the letter below and pay particular attention to learning the highlighted phrases. It would be a good idea to try to learn the booking letter by heart!

This letter can be adapted by putting in different rooms, requirements and dates. It could also be used to book in at a campsite (see the Notes/Options 12).

Bath
le 20 avril

Monsieur / Madame,

Je voudrais réserver[1] deux chambres à votre hôtel **du** 8 août **au** 10 août[2]. Je voudrais une chambre **avec un grand lit**[3] avec douche et une chambre **à deux lits**[4] avec salle de bains.

Est-ce que vous pouvez m'indiquer vos prix[5] et **m'envoyer une brochure sur l'hôtel**?[6]

Est-ce qu'il y a[7] un restaurant à l'hôtel? **J'arriverai**[8] le 8 août à 17 h. **Je vous envoie des arrhes de** 50 **€.**[9]

J'attends confirmation de votre part.[10]

Veuillez agréer, Monsieur / Madame, l'expression de mes sentiments distingués.

1 I'd like to reserve
2 from + date / to + date
3 with a double bed
4 with two single beds
5 Can you let me know your prices?
6 and send me a brochure about the hotel.
7 Is there a
8 I'll be arriving
9 I'm sending a deposit of
10 I await your confirmation

- To book at a youth hostel for two boys and two girls you would need to ask: **Avez-vous de la place pour deux garçons et deux filles?** (change details as necessary). You would still need to give details of dates, times of arrival and you may want to ask questions about facilities (see Notes/Options 12 and 13).

A reply from a hotel

Hôtel du Parc
le 29 avril

Monsieur,

En réponse à votre lettre[1], dont nous vous remercions vivement, c'est **avec plaisir que nous vous confirmons votre réservation**[2] de deux chambres du 8 au 10 août.

Veuillez trouver ci-joint nos tarifs[3] et un dépliant sur l'hôtel. **Je confirme**[4] qu'il y a un restaurant à l'hôtel.

Nous avons bien reçu vos arrhes pour un montant de 50€[5].

Dans l'attente du plaisir de vous accueillir, nous vous prions d'agréer, Monsieur, l'assurance de nos sentiments dévoués.

Sabrine Blanquet

Directrice

1 In reply to your letter

2 We are pleased to confirm your reservation

3 Please find enclosed our prices

4 I confirm

5 We have received your deposit for the sum of 50€.

16 Monsieur / Madame	= Dear Sir / Madam *– Never start a formal letter with* **Cher** *or* **Chère**! *These are equivalents of Dear, as in loved one.*
Veuillez agréer, Monsieur / Madame, l'expression de mes sentiments distingués.	= Yours sincerely / faithfully, *– This is the formal way of signing off. It appears flowery to us, but it is French style!*
Dans l'attente du plaisir de vous accueillir.	= We look forward to welcoming you. *– Note the formal signing off used often by hotels – don't use this one yourself.*
Je regrette mais on est complet.	= I am sorry but we are full.
17 Qu'est-ce qu'il y a à faire / voir dans la ville / région?	= What is there to do/ see in the town / region?

Test yourself

Task 1 **Writing**

Write a letter of reservation to a French hotel.

- Ask for 2 rooms for 2 people with shower.

- Give the dates (eg 16–31 August).
- Ask for information about prices.
- Say you are sending 50€ as a deposit.

Remember to use the booking letter on page 26 for some help, and even copy phrases from it if you get stuck!

Task 2 **Speaking**

Here's a role play exercise.

You are booking in at a French hotel.

1 Ask if there are rooms available.

2 Say you would like a room with two beds.

3 Say you would like a shower.

4 Say it is for 3 nights.

5 Ask how much it is.

Now try the role play again changing the room details and number of nights. Ask if there is a TV in the room or a swimming-pool at the hotel.

Task 3 **Writing**

Prepare an e-mail to a campsite in France. Give the following information:

- tent or caravan?

- number of people

- dates

Ask

- the prices
- if there is a pool

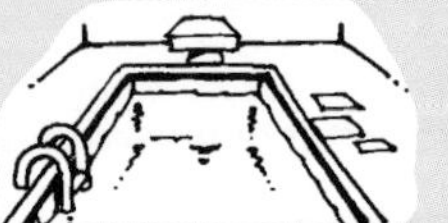

Task 4 **Reading**

Lisez cette annonce.

CAMPING LES CRIQUES * NN**

Piscine – Jeux d'enfants – Restaurant – Parking

Salle de télévision – Douches – Emplacements à l'ombre – Boulangerie

Animaux non admis 68 emplacements (tentes)

Tel 04-68-12-73-96 1 avril – 30 septembre

Qu'est-ce qu'il y a au camping?

Cochez les cases appropriées (✓).

Exemple

Going for a C?

Listen to the CD (Chapter 4 Foundation). Listen twice.

Ecoutez la conversation à l'hôtel. Notez les détails en français et cochez les cases appropriées. Ecoutez deux fois.

Réservation

1. NOM ....
2. Détails des chambres: 2 chambre(s)
   Une chambre avec .... lit(s)
   Une chambre avec .... lit(s)
3. Salle de bains ou douche? ....
4. Pour .... nuits.
5. Restaurant: ouvert de .... h à .... h ....
6. Piscine: ouvert de .... h à .... h
7. Terrain de jeux: oui ❑ non ❑
8. Parking – où? ....
9. Numéros des chambres .... et ....

Answers

TASK 2

1 Avez-vous des chambres?
2 Je voudrais une chambre à deux lits.
3 Avec douche.
4 C'est pour 3 nuits.
5 C'est combien?

TASK 4

✓ for 1, 2, 4, 5, 7, 11, 12 = 7 points

Answers

Going for a C?

1 CARDINAL
2 une chambre à un lit, une chambre à 2 lits
3 salle de bains
4 3 nuits
5 7h à 9h30 / 9h et demie
6 9h - 6h
7 oui
8 derrière l'hôtel
9 110 and 111

Take a break

Now look back at the Checklist on page 24 – you should now be feeling fine for all of the questions. If not spend ten minutes looking at the word lists on pages 89–90. Copy out ten words or phrases you find hard to remember. Then spend your time focusing on the ten words – that will make the best use of your time!

For your own notes

Vous avez → have you

Je peux → Can I

Checklist

How do you feel about these?
In French, can you:

		Fine	Help!
1	answer the questions on the Foundation Checklist on page 24?	❑	❑

If you've ticked the Help! box, go back to the Foundation Notes/Options and revise!

At a hotel

		Fine	Help!
2	cope with more unexpected elements, such as mistaken identity, incorrect reservation details, losing a key, accidents in the room?	❑	❑
3	make more detailed complaints, such as about the lack of facilities or too much noise?	❑	❑
4	write a letter of complaint to a hotel and explain the problem?	❑	❑

Where are you staying?

Break any topic you revise into smaller, more manageable parts, e.g. think of 'hotel' as – 1. what kind of room? 2. what facilities in the hotel? 3. when things go wrong. Imagine actually arriving at a hotel: be creative and feel free to use language from other topics. Picturing the situation will help you remember the phrases better.

Help is at hand!

Notes/Options

1 Check back to the Foundation Checklist. If you feel confident, carry on!

2	Vous vous êtes trompé(e).	= You have made a mistake.
	Je ne suis pas M. Brown. Je suis M. Woods.	= I'm not Mr Brown. = I'm Mr Woods.
	J'ai réservé deux chambres la semaine dernière.	= I reserved two rooms last week.
	Je voulais une chambre avec douche.	= I wanted a room with a shower.
	Je voulais seulement une chambre.	= I wanted only one room.
	Je vous ai écrit – voici votre lettre de confirmation.	= I wrote to you, here is your letter of confirmation.
	Je vous ai envoyé un fax / un e-mail.	= I sent you a fax / an e-mail.
	J'ai déjà versé des arrhes.	= I've already paid a deposit.
	La note n'est pas correcte.	= The bill is wrong.
	J'ai perdu ma clé – je suis désolé(e).	= I've lost my key – I'm sorry.
	J'ai cassé la lampe / la télévision.	= I've broken the lamp / TV.
	J'ai renversé du lait / du vin.	= I've spilt some milk / some wine.
3	Je ne peux pas dormir – il y a trop de bruit.	= I can't sleep – there's too much noise.
	J'ai eu froid hier soir. Il n'y avait pas de couvertures dans la chambre.	= I was cold last night. There were no blankets in the room.
	L'eau est froide.	= The water is cold.
4	Le service était affreux.	= The service was awful.
	Les garçons n'étaient pas polis.	= The waiters were impolite.
	Les repas étaient froids.	= The meals were cold.
	Le chauffage ne marchait pas.	= The heating wasn't working.
	Il y avait beaucoup de bruit.	= There was a lot of noise.
	La salle de bains était sale.	= The bathroom was dirty.
	J'espère que vous ne tarderez pas à me rembourser une partie du prix de séjour.	= I hope that you will not delay in repaying part of the cost to me.

Going for an A?

Read this letter making sure you understand all of the points and then you can memorise the key phrases.

A letter of complaint

6 Waterborne Road
LONDON
SW17 4JP

le 29 août

Monsieur Casé
Directeur
Hôtel de la Place

Monsieur,

J'ai le regret de vous informer que je ne suis pas du tout satisfait(e) de mon séjour à votre hôtel (du 20 au 23 août). Le service était affreux – au restaurant, les garçons n'étaient pas très polis et les repas étaient froids.

J'ai passé une nuit très fatigante dans ma chambre. Le chauffage ne marchait pas et à cause d'une soirée disco à l'hôtel il y a avait beaucoup de bruit. La salle de bains était sale et j'ai dû demander une serviette propre.

J'espère que vous ne tarderez pas à me rembourser une partie du prix de séjour.

Veuillez agréer, Monsieur, mes salutations distinguées.

Alex Hanson.

Test yourself

Task 1 **Listening**

Listen to the CD (Chapter 4 Higher). Play it twice.

Ecoutez les quatre conversations.

Pour chaque conversation (1–4) notez le problème en français.

Ecoutez le CD deux fois.

Exemple 1 – le chauffage ne marche pas.

Task 2 **Writing**

Vous avez passé un mauvais séjour à un hôtel. Ecrivez une lettre (120 mots) au directeur / à la directrice. Décrivez les problèmes. Demandez un remboursement.

Use the model letter to help!

Check back to the letter and correct your mistakes.

Task 3 **Reading**

Read the following article which gives advice about what to do if your rented holiday accommodation is not up to standard. Answer the questions in English.

Votre location de vacances ne vous convient pas? La maison avec 'vue sur la mer' donne sur un parking et le trois-pièces n'est qu'un studio? Quels sont vos droits? Que faut-il faire?

Dès votre arrivée faites la liste des éléments incorrects et adoptez une stratégie.

Vous restez ... avec une réduction.

- Demandez une réduction du prix de la location. Si le propriétaire vous fait la sourde oreille téléphonez à l'office du tourisme.
- Adressez un courrier à la commission départementale de l'action touristique qui effectuera une visite de contrôle.
- Si vous avez loué par l'intermédiaire d'un organisme (Gîtes de France ...) contactez le responsable qui trouvera un accord aimable avec le propriétaire.

Vous partez: exigez d'être remboursé. Si vous partez demandez le remboursement des sommes déjà payées. Si vous avez versé des arrhes vous avez le droit de demander le double de la somme.

Les négociations se passent mal? Avant de porter plainte auprès du Procureur de la République n'oubliez pas ...

- que vous pouvez faire appel à un témoin.
- de prendre des photos de la propriété pour faire valoir vos droits.
- de faire une copie de votre contrat.

1 What should you do as soon as you arrive?

2 If you decide to stay, what should you ask the owner to do?

3 If the owner is unco-operative where should you ring for help?

4 If you rent a property through a company or agency (e.g. Gîtes de France), what should you do?

5 If you decide to leave, what should you ask the owner to do?

6 If you have given the owner a deposit, what can you ask for?

7 What should you do before you make a complaint to a public prosecutor (Procureur de la République)?

Answers

TASK 1

2 Le repas était froid – le service était affreux, les garçons étaient impolis.

3 La chambre est sale. Il n'y a pas de serviettes dans la salle de bains.

4 La note n'est pas correcte (le client n'a pas mangé à l'hôtel).

TASK 3

1 Make a list of things which aren't right.

2 Give you a reduction.

3 The Tourist Office.

4 Contact the person in charge at that agency / there.

5 Refund any money already paid.

6 Ask for double the amount of the deposit.

7 Get a witness, take photos of the property, make a copy of the contract.

For your own notes

....

....

....

....

....

....

....

....

Checklist

How do you feel about these?
In French, can you:

		Fine	Help!
1	say how many weeks' school holidays you have a year and name the holidays?	❑	❑
2	say where you normally go on holiday?	❑	❑
3	say who you go with?	❑	❑
4	say for how long you go?	❑	❑
5	say what you do on holiday?	❑	❑
6	ask other people for the above information?	❑	❑
7	say how you travel?	❑	❑
	Describe a recent holiday		
8	say where you went, who you went with and how you travelled?	❑	❑
9	say what the weather was like?	❑	❑
10	say what you did and saw?	❑	❑
11	give simple opinions about the holiday?	❑	❑
12	talk about holiday plans for your next holiday?	❑	❑
13	ask for details about a town or region you want to visit as a tourist?	❑	❑

Describing a holiday

This is another favourite topic of conversation! The word lists on pages 91–93 will help you to memorise the key vocabulary about what you do on holiday, where you go and so on. Note you can use the same phrases in the past and future tenses – you only have to change the verb form. So you get twice the benefit from learning the language!

HELP IS AT HAND!

		Notes/Options
1	Tu as combien de semaines de vacances scolaires?	
	J'ai deux semaines à Noël, une semaine pour les vacances du mi-trimestre, deux semaines à Pâques, une semaine en mai, six semaines pour les grandes vacances et une semaine en octobre.	Noël = Christmas mi-trimestre= half term Pâques = Easter
2	D'habitude où vas-tu en vacances?	d'habitude = normally
	Normalement, je vais au bord de la mer.	= to the seaside
	à la montagne	= to the mountains
	à la campagne	= to the country *– Remember to use the present tense. For example:* Je vais au bord de la mer.
	Tu restes / descends à l'hôtel?	= Do you stay in a hotel?
	Oui, je descends à l'hôtel.	= Yes, I stay in a hotel.
	Non, on loue un gîte ou un appartement.	= No, we hire a holiday cottage or a flat.
	Non, je séjourne dans un appartement / une maison de vacances.	= No, I stay in a holiday flat / house.
	Non, je vais au camping.	= No, I go to a campsite.
	On va à l'auberge de jeunesse.	= We go to a youth hostel.
	Non, je fais du camping.	= No, I go camping.
	Tu restes en Angleterre ou tu vas à l'étranger?	à l'étranger = abroad
	Je vais à l'étranger. Je vais en France / en Espagne.	
	Je vais à Paris / à Madrid.	*– Use* **à** *with the name of a town or city.*
	Je reste en Angleterre.	= I stay in England.
	Je vais à Swanage.	= I go to Swanage.

Mes vacances – Foundation

3 Avec qui est-ce que tu pars en vacances? Je vais en vacances avec mes amis. Je pars en vacances avec ma famille.	= Who do you go on holiday with?
4 Tu pars pour combien de temps? Je pars pour une semaine / huit jours. une quinzaine	= a week / seven days = a fortnight
Pendant combien de temps?	= For how long?
Pendant deux semaines / quinze jours.	= For two weeks / a fortnight.
5 Que fais-tu pendant tes vacances?	

See the word list on page 91 for some more ideas.

Je fais de la natation, je joue au tennis et je vais à la plage.	
Je fais du shopping / du lèche-vitrines.	= I go shopping / window shopping.
Je me bronze / Je visite la région.	= I sunbathe / I visit the region.
Je me promène / Je fais des promenades.	= I go for walks.

6 Make sure you know all the questions from 1–4 on the Checklist so that you can ask other people about their holidays.

7 Comment voyages-tu?	= How do you travel?
Je voyage en bateau.	= I travel by boat.
Je vais en avion.	= I travel by plane.
en voiture	= by car
en train	= by train
en car	= by coach
Le voyage prend combien de temps?	= How long does the journey take?
Le voyage dure ...	= The journey lasts ...
Ça prend cinq heures.	= It takes five hours.

– *All these Notes/Options require the present tense.*

For the following Notes/Options you need the perfect tense. (See page 109.)

8 Où es-tu allé(e) l'année dernière, pendant les grandes vacances?	= Where did you go last year during the main / summer holidays?
Je suis allé(e) en France, au bord de la mer.	je suis allé(e) = I went
Tu es allé(e) avec qui?	= Who did you go with?
Tu es allé(e) en vacances avec tes ami(e)s? Non, je suis allé(e) avec ma famille.	= Did you go with your friends?
Tu es descendu(e) à l'hôtel?	=Did you stay at a hotel?
Non, j'ai passé mes vacances dans un appartement.	= No, I spent my holiday in a flat.
Oui, j'ai passé mes vacances à l'hôtel.	= Yes, I spent my holidays at a hotel.
Oui, je suis descendu(e) à l'hôtel.	= Yes, I stayed at a hotel.
Comment as-tu voyagé?	
J'ai voyagé en bateau et en voiture.	J'ai voyagé = I travelled
9 Quel temps faisait-il pendant ton séjour?	= What was the weather like during your stay?

– *Note that* faisait *is a past tense – the imperfect tense. See the Grammar page 130 for more help on the imperfect.*

The word list on page 92 includes weather phrases.

Il faisait beau / soleil / chaud / froid.	= The weather was fine / sunny / hot / cold.
Il pleuvait.	= It was rainy.
Il faisait de l'orage.	= The weather was stormy.
10 Qu'est-ce que tu as fait pendant les vacances?	= What did you do during the holidays?
J'ai nagé, j'ai joué au tennis et je suis sorti(e) avec mes amis.	= I swam, I played tennis and I went out with my friends.
Je me suis bronzé(e).	= I sunbathed.
J'ai fait la grasse-matinée.	= I got up late.
Je me suis promené(e).	= I went for walks.
J'ai acheté des souvenirs.	= I bought some souvenirs.
Qu'est-ce que tu as vu?	
J'ai visité des monuments historiques, j'ai visité la ville et un parc de loisirs.	

11 Qu'est-ce que tu as pensé de tes vacances?	= What did you think of your holidays?
J'ai adoré les vacances.	= I loved my holidays.
Je me suis bien amusé(e).	= I had a good time.
J'ai aimé la nourriture et les gens.	= I liked the food and the people.
Je n'ai pas aimé la nourriture.	= I didn't like the food.

– *See the Higher section of this chapter for more opinions.*

Make sure you can ask the Checklist 7–12 so that you can ask other people what they did.

12 Quels sont tes projets de vacances pour cet été?	= What are your holiday plans for this summer?

Remember, to talk about future plans, use either the future tense (see pages 112 and 130) or use **je vais** + the infinitive to say what you are going to do.

Look carefully at the future tense phrases on page 91 to handle the question in Notes/Options point 12.

13 Je voudrais des renseignements sur la ville.	= I would like some information about the town.

Going for a C?

Remember, examiners will expect to hear what you do normally (present tense), what you did (perfect tense) and what you will do (future tense). Holidays is one of the best topics to show off how well you can do in the different time zones.

Record yourself reading out the Checklist from 1–7. Then record your answers.

Then do the same for 8–11.

Finally prepare your complete answer to 12 – as if you were in the exam!

Test yourself

Task 1 **Speaking**

Use the cue card below and try to talk for about two minutes on **Mes vacances.**

Refer to the Notes/Options if you get stuck.

Mes vacances

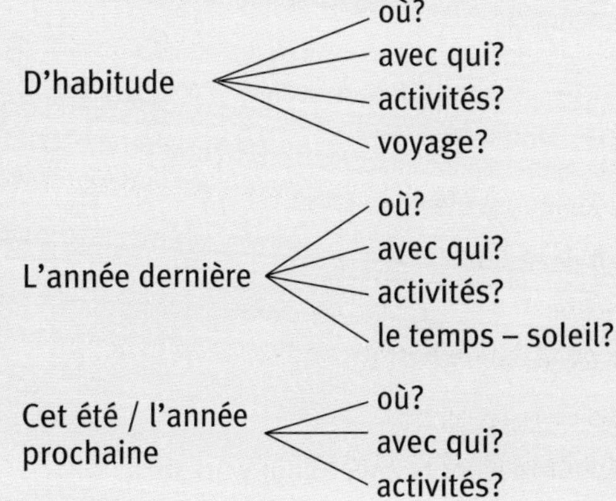

Task 2 **Writing**

You are on holiday in France. Write a postcard in French (40 words) to a French friend. Say

- Where you are staying.

- Who you are with.

- What the weather is like.

- What you are doing.

Task 3 **Writing**

Write a reply to Anne-Marie's letter.

le 2 septembre

Salut!

Comment vas-tu? As-tu passé de bonnes vacances? Où es-tu allé(e) et avec qui? Qu'est-ce que tu as visité?

Veux-tu venir en France à Noël? Je suis libre du 20 décembre au 3 janvier.

Réponds-moi vite.

Amitiés

Anne-Marie

Ask your teacher to check your work for accuracy. Don't be too ambitious – write only what you know how to say!

Remember to spot the questions in the letter; you must answer each question asked to get communication marks in the exam.

Task 4 **Writing**

You want to visit the town of Béziers. Write a letter to the tourist office.

Ask for

- brochures
- a town plan
- information about what there is to visit

Ask questions about

- when market day is
- the shop opening times

une brochure	= a brochure
un dépliant	= a leaflet
un plan	= a plan
une carte	= a map
une liste d'appartements à louer	= a list of flats to rent
une liste de restaurants	= a list of restaurants

When you've finished, check your letter back against the model letter on this page.

Est-ce qu'il y a un musée?	= Is there a museum?
Qu'est-ce qu'on peut faire à Collioure?	= What can one do/is there to do in Collioure?
Quels sont les jours de marché?	= When are the market days?
Qu'est-ce qu'il y a à visiter?	= What is there to visit?
A quelle heure ferment les magasins?	= When do the shops close?
Quelle est la date de la fête régionale?	= When is the local festival day?

Going for a C?

How would you ask for details about a town or region you are planning to visit?

12 Fir Road
Hereford
Angleterre

le 5 mai

Syndicat d'Initiative
Collioure
France

Monsieur,

Je vous serais très obligé(e) si[1] **vous pourriez m'envoyer**[2] des informations sur la ville de Collioure. **Veuillez m'envoyer**[3] des brochures, un plan de la ville, une liste d'hôtels et une liste d'appartements à louer, s'il vous plaît. **Je voudrais aussi savoir**[4] **ce qu'il y a à faire**[5] dans la ville. Est-ce qu'il y a des monuments à visiter?

Veuillez trouver ci-joint une enveloppe pour la réponse.[6]

Je vous remercie d'avance.[7]

Veuillez agréer, Monsieur, l'expression de mes sentiments distingués.[8]

Sue Davidson

1 I would be grateful if
2 you could send me
3 Please send me
4 I would also like to know
5 what there is to do
6 Please find enclosed an envelope for reply
7 Thanking you in advance
8 Yours faithfully

Checklist

How do you feel about these?
In French, can you:

	Fine	Help!
1 answer the questions on the Foundation Checklist on page 33?	❑	❑
If you've ticked the Help! box, go back to the Foundation Notes/Options and revise!		
2 give fuller details about places visited or holiday plans?	❑	❑
3 express opinions and make judgements about places visited and holiday activities?	❑	❑

Describing a holiday

This is another favourite topic of conversation! The word lists on pages 91–93 will help you to memorise the key vocabulary about what you do on holiday, where you go and so on. Note you can use the same phrases in the past and future tenses – you only have to change the verb form. So you get twice the benefit from learning the language!

Help is at hand!

Notes/Options

1 Once you've looked back at the Foundation Checklist on page 33 and you feel confident – carry on!

2 Fuller details means that you must be able to give more than one or two factual details. You should be able to talk and write about your holidays in the past, present and future tenses using the correct time zone markers.

Perfect	Present	Future
L'année dernière ...	D'habitude ... Normalement ...	Cet été ... L'année prochaine ...
je suis allé(e)	je vais	j'irai
je suis resté(e)	je reste	je resterai
j'ai passé	je passe	je passerai
j'ai pris l'avion	je prends l'avion	je prendrai l'avion
je suis sorti(e)	je sors	je sortirai

Continue these three lists using verbs in the three tenses. Draw a spider diagram for each time zone putting in the correct forms of the verbs. The word lists on pages 109–112 will help you.

See Notes/Options 3 for more expressions.

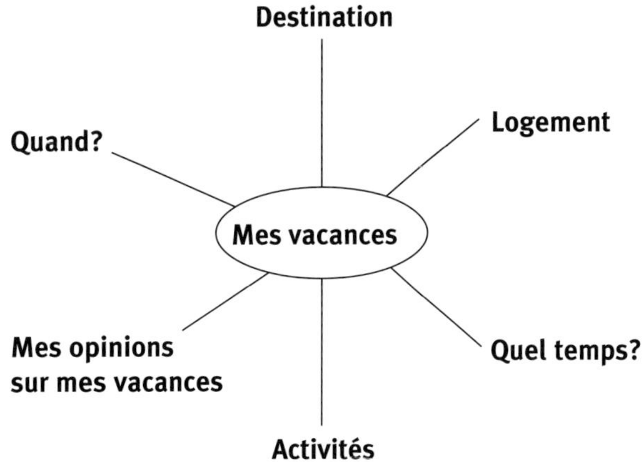

The difference between the Foundation cue card in Task 1 on page 35 and the above cue card is in the amount of extra detail you can provide and the variety of verbs you can use correctly without guidance from the examiner.

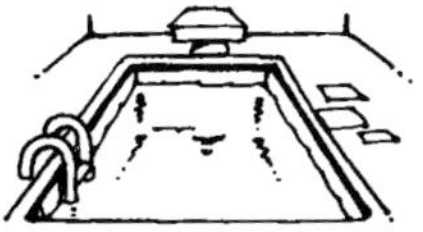

3 Here are some useful opinions about holiday trips – some positive and some negative. Use a dictionary to help check the meanings if you are stuck!

* Remember **parce que** becomes **parce qu'** before a vowel.

POSITIVE

J'ai aimé mon séjour parce que / qu'
c'était différent

- c'était intéressant
- la nourriture était délicieuse
- il faisait plus chaud qu'en Angleterre*
- les gens étaient sympa
- les gens étaient accueillants
- j'étais souvent avec mes ami(e)s
- le paysage était très beau
- j'ai visité beaucoup de choses

NEGATIVE

Je n'ai pas aimé mon séjour parce que / qu'
c'était ennuyeux

- ce n'était pas intéressant
- la nourriture était affreuse
- il faisait trop chaud*
- les gens n'étaient pas sympa
- les gens n'étaient pas accueillants
- j'étais souvent avec mes parents(!)
- le paysage était sans intérêt
- j'ai visité trop de monuments

Going for an A?

Mes vacances idéales. Try to use the conditional tense (see page 131) to describe where you would spend your dream holidays.

Start off
Si j'étais riche
Si j'avais beaucoup d'argent
Si j'avais assez de temps

j'irais	= I would go
je passerais un mois	= I would spend a month ...
je resterais	= I would stay
je nagerais	= I would swim
je mangerais	= I would eat
je sortirais	= I would go out
je visiterais	= I would visit
je serais	= I would be

Remember that holidays and trips to France are frequently discussed and tested in examinations, so make sure that you can cope with the different tenses.

Remember that examiners are looking for opinions and reasons why.

For your own notes

....

....

....

....

....

....

....

....

Test yourself

Task 1 Speaking

Have a go at telling the story, making use of the prompts and the pictures. When you have finished, listen to the CD (Chapter 5, Higher) to hear a model answer.

The notes and pictures below give an outline of the beginning of an exchange trip to France last year.

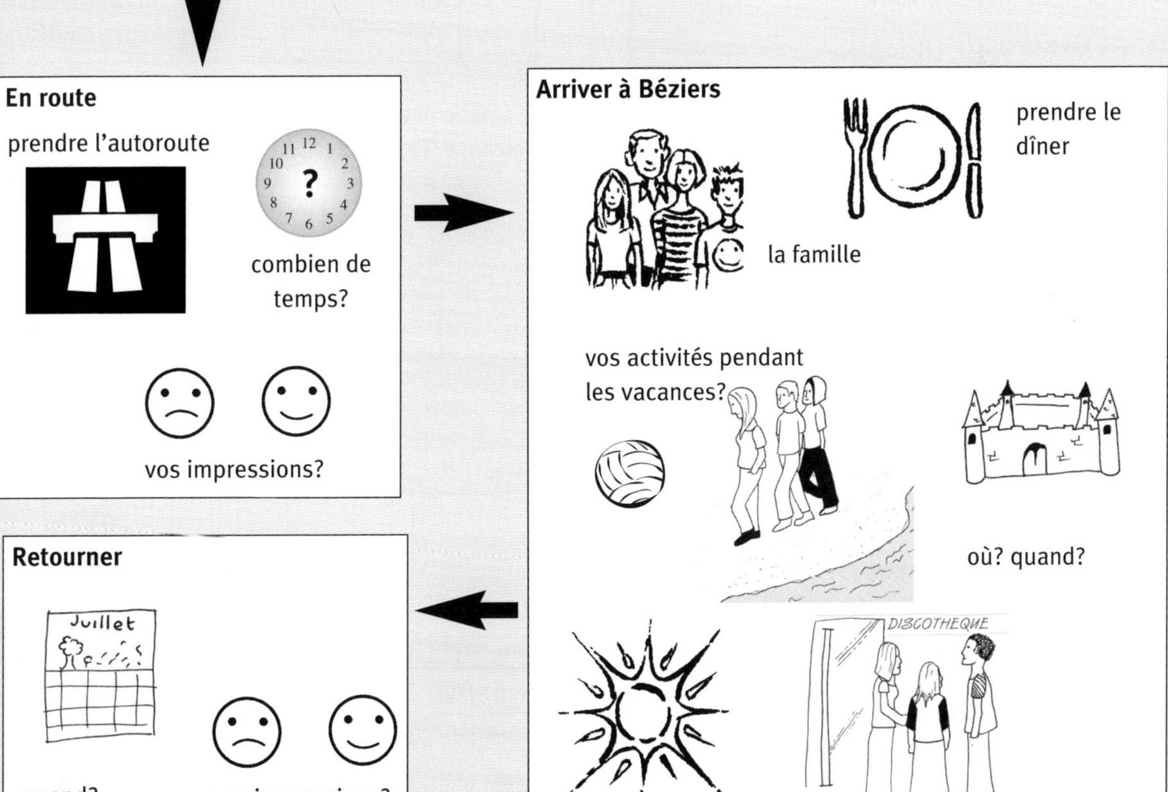

Checklist

How do you feel about these?
In French, can you:

		Fine	Help!
1	give a simple description of your home town and surrounding area?	❑	❑
2	say what there is to do there (including festivals)?	❑	❑
3	give simple opinions about your town?	❑	❑
4	ask where a place is?	❑	❑
5	say how to get to a place?	❑	❑
6	understand directions given to you?	❑	❑
7	give and understand information about public transport (bus, coach, train, underground)?	❑	❑
8	understand simple signs and notices?	❑	❑
9	buy tickets (destination, single / return, class)?	❑	❑
10	buy fuel for a car and ask the cost?	❑	❑
11	ask for the water, oil and tyres to be checked?	❑	❑
12	give simple details about a breakdown?	❑	❑
13	understand and describe weather conditions?	❑	❑

Out and about

Work through the word lists on pages 94–95. You'll find these most helpful not only for your exams, but also when you're travelling around France. Throughout this chapter, imagine yourself in all the situations: be creative and expand on the phrases given, using language from other other areas.

Help is at hand!

		Notes/Options
1	Décris-moi ta ville / ton village.	
	C'est une grande / petite ville.	
	il y a des usines	= there are factories
	Elle est moderne / industrielle / historique / touristique / administrative.	
	Il y a des monuments historiques.	= There are historical monuments.
	Où se trouve ta ville / ton village?	
	C'est dans le nord de l'Angleterre.	le sud / l'est / l'ouest
	C'est à 100 kilomètres de Birmingham.	= It's 100 kilometres from Birmingham.
	C'est à une heure de Leeds.	= It's an hour from Leeds.
	Il y a quinze mille habitants.	= There are 15,000 inhabitants.
2	Qu'est-ce qu'il y a comme distractions dans ta ville?	= What kinds of leisure facilities are there in your town?
	pour les jeunes	= for young people
	pour les touristes	= for the tourists
	Qu'est-ce qu'on peut faire dans ta ville?	= What can one / you do in your town?

Il y a	une piscine, un terrain de football, de grands magasins, un centre commercial, un jardin public, un parc, un théâtre, un cinéma, une bibliothèque, un centre sportif, des monuments historiques, une cathédrale

– *Be prepared to talk about festivals in your town! For example:* Il y a un festival d'art / de danse / de musique. On chante et on danse.

On peut	visiter les magasins aller au festival de jazz aller à la discothèque / aller au théâtre faire du sport / des excursions faire du tourisme

3 Que penses-tu de ta ville?

POSITIVE
J'aime ma ville! C'est intéressant! / C'est chouette! Il y a beaucoup à faire.

NEGATIVE
Je n'aime pas ma ville! C'est ennuyeux! / C'est moche! Il n'y a rien à faire.

4 Où se trouve / est le jardin public?	= Where is the park?
la bibliothèque	= the library
le centre commercial	= the shopping centre
5/6 Pour aller à la gare s'il vous plaît?	= How do I get to the station, please?

See the phrases on page 94 about how to get to places in a town. Visualise your own town: draw a symbol for ten places, and write a sentence asking the way to each one.

Tournez à droite / à gauche.	= Turn to the right / left.
Continuez tout droit.	= Carry straight on.
Prenez la première rue à droite.	= Take the first road on the right.
traversez le pont	= cross the bridge
c'est après les feux / le rond-point	= it's after the lights / the roundabout
C'est loin? Non c'est près d'ici.	= Is it far? No it's nearby.
Prenez le bus numéro cinq, voilà l'arrêt d'autobus.	= Take the number five bus, there's the bus stop.
7 A quelle heure part le prochain train / car pour Paris?	= When does the next train / coach leave for Paris?
Il y un car pour Paris?	= Is there a coach to Paris?
A quelle heure arrive le train à Paris?	= When does the train arrive in Paris?
Le voyage prend combien de temps?	= How long does the trip take?
Ça prendra combien de temps?	= How long will it take?
Est-ce qu'il faut changer?	= Do I have to change trains?
C'est direct?	= Is it direct?
Il y a une correspondance?	= Is there a connection?
C'est quelle ligne? (métro)	= Which line is it? (underground)
la gare / la gare routière	= the railway / bus station
la station de métro	underground station
8 Attention!	= Watch out!

Many of the signs you see in France are obvious to English speakers. Have a look at the word list on page 95 for the less obvious signs you need to know.

9 Buying a train ticket.	
un aller-retour	= return ticket
un aller simple	= one-way ticket
en première classe / en deuxième classe	= in first class / in second class
Ça coûte combien?	= How much is it?

Je voudrais un carnet s'il vous plaît.	un carnet = a book of ten tickets un ticket = one ticket. Quel quai? = Which platform?
Le train part de quel quai? De quel quai part le train?	= Which platform does the train leave from?
C'est quel quai?	Which platform is it? le quai = la voie *– Both words can be used at a railway station.* la voie = the track
10 A la station service	= At the petrol station
Faites le plein s'il vous plaît.	= Fill it up, please.
Gazole ou essence?	le gazole = diesel l'essence = petrol
Du sans plomb 98. sans plomb 95 super	= unleaded = unleaded = LRP
11 Vous désirez autre chose?	
Oui, un litre d'huile.	= Yes, a litre of oil.
Avez-vous une carte routière?	= Have you got a road map?
Où sont les toilettes?	= Where are the toilets?
Vous vendez des boissons?	= Do you sell drinks?
Voulez-vous vérifier les pneus / l'huile / l'eau?	= Would you check the tyres / oil / water?
C'est bien la route pour Dijon?	= Is this the right road to Dijon?

12	Je suis tombé(e) en panne.	= I've broken down (about a car!).
	Le moteur ne marche pas.	= The engine isn't working.
	Les freins ne marchent pas.	= The brakes aren't working.
	J'ai crevé / un pneu est crevé.	= I've had a puncture.
	C'est quelle marque de voiture?	= What make of car is it?
	C'est une Ford.	= It's a Ford.
	Quel est le numéro d'immatriculation?	= What is the registration number?
	C'est WR 05 VXG.	*– Be prepared to give numbers and spell out the letters!*
	Je suis à cinq kilomètres de Dijon.	= I'm five kilometres from Dijon.
	une autoroute	= a motorway
	une route nationale	= a main road (like an A-road)
13	Il pleut à verse!	It's pouring with rain!

For the complete scene on the weather front, look at the word list on page 92. Describe your favourite weather and your most dreaded weather. Draw a symbol for each.

Going for a C?

Learn the vocabulary below to help you understand weather forecasts.

agréable	= pleasant
une averse	= a shower
le climat	= the climate
la chute	= the drop (in temperature)
degré	= degree
demain	= tomorrow
un éclair	= a flash of lightning
une éclaircie	= a sunny spell
fort	= strong
léger	= light
meilleur	= better
la pluie	= the rain
plus tard	= later on
les prévisions	= forecasts
prochain	= next
rapidement	= quickly
la température	= the temperature
... basse / haute	= ... low / high
Quel temps fait-il?	= What's the weather like?

Test yourself

Task 1 **Speaking**

Cue card

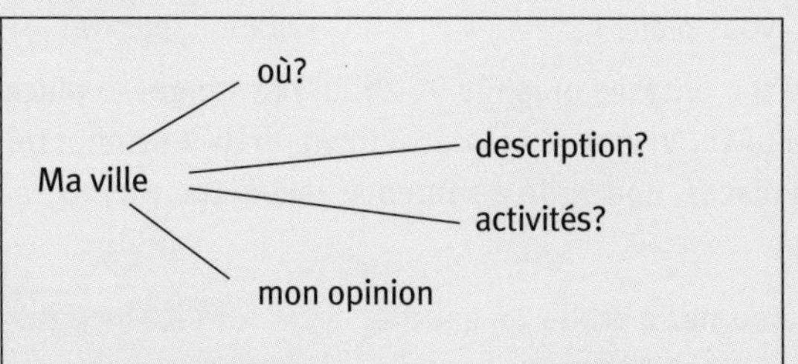

You should be getting really good at talking for one minute on a subject. Try talking about the town where you live.

Use the cue card and Notes/Options 1–3.

Task 2 **Speaking**

Here's a role play exercise. Imagine that you are at Dijon railway station and want to go to Paris.

1

Ask when the next train to Paris leaves.

2

Ask when the train arrives in Paris.

3

Ask for a single ticket to Paris.

4

Ask how much it is.

5

Ask which platform it is.

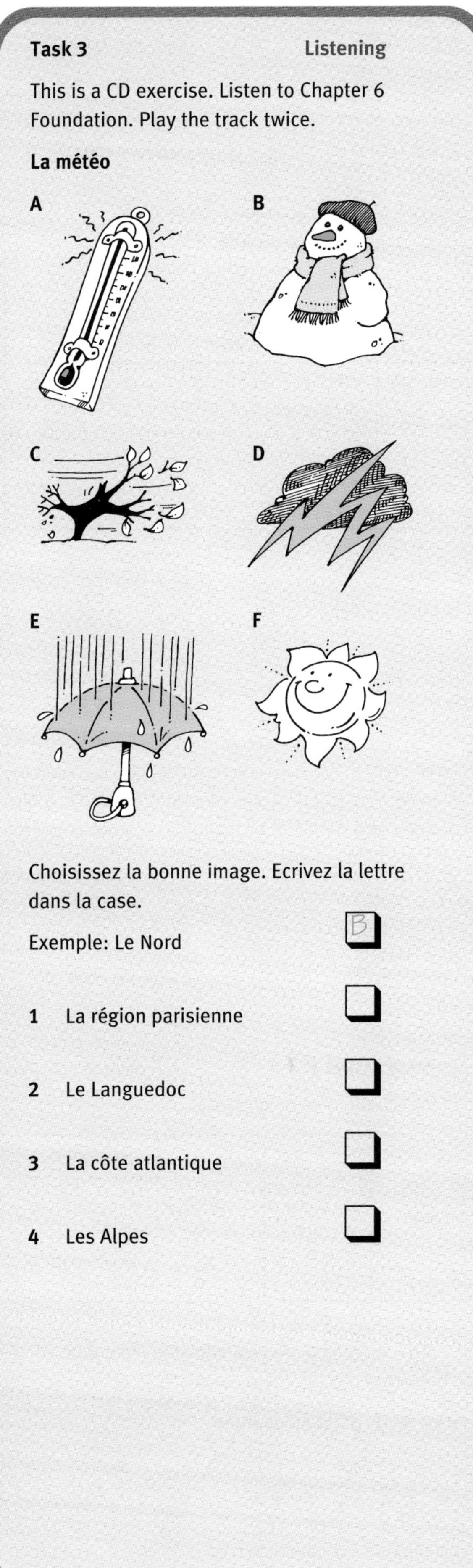

Task 3 **Listening**

This is a CD exercise. Listen to Chapter 6 Foundation. Play the track twice.

La météo

A B C D E F

Choisissez la bonne image. Ecrivez la lettre dans la case.

Exemple: Le Nord B

1 La région parisienne

2 Le Languedoc

3 La côte atlantique

4 Les Alpes

Task 4 **Reading**

Choisissez la bonne lettre (A–H) pour chaque numéro (1–6).

Exemple: Le buffet = B

1 Salle d'attente =

2 Non fumeur =

3 Toilettes (femmes) =

4 Sortie =

5 Consigne =

6 Guichets =

A B C D E Billets F WC G H

Task 5 **Writing**

Write a letter (80 words) to your French friend about your town.

- Describe your town
- Say what there is to do
- Give your opinion about where you live

Use the Notes/Options to check your work.

Answers

TASK 2

1 A quelle heure part le prochain train pour Paris?
2 A quelle heure arrive le train à Paris?
3 Je voudrais un aller simple à Paris.
4 C'est combien?
5 C'est quel quai?

TASK 3

1 E, 2 F, 3 C, 4 D

TASK 4

1 G, 2 H, 3 F, 4 A, 5 C, 6 E

Checklist

How do you feel about these?
In French, can you:

		Fine	Help!
1	answer the questions on the Foundation Checklist on page 40?	❑	❑

If you've ticked the Help! box, go back to the Foundation Notes/Options and revise!

2	understand and make comparisons between your country and a French-speaking country (towns, geo-graphical features, climate)?	❑	❑
3	express and explain opinions about where you live?	❑	❑
4	describe important local festivals?	❑	❑
5	explain your preferences about travel?	❑	❑
6	report an accident (giving location and details)?	❑	❑

Out and about

Work through the word lists on pages 94–95. You'll find these most helpful not only for your exams, but also when you're travelling around France. Throughout this chapter, imagine yourself in all the situations: be creative and expand on the phrases given, using language from other other areas.

HELP IS AT HAND!

Notes/Options

1 Once you've looked back at the Foundation Checklist and you feel confident – carry on!

2 plus ... que = more than
moins ... que = less than
Le climat est plus / moins humide / sec qu'ici. = The climate is more/ less humid / dry than here.
chaud(e)
froid(e)
meilleur(e)
Le paysage est plus / moins beau / vallonné. = The countryside is more / less beautiful / hilly.
La région est plus / moins plate / verte. = The region is more / less flat / green.
intéressant(e) = interesting
montagneux/euse = mountainous

3 Quels sont les avantages et les inconvénients de ta ville?

J'aime / Je n'aime pas habiter chez moi ...

parce qu'	il fait trop chaud / froid il y a beaucoup à faire il n'y a rien à faire il y a trop de bruit / de pollution
parce que	j'habite trop loin des distractions / de mes amis le soir il n'y a pas de transport public - il est difficile de rentrer c'est une belle ville c'est une ville sans intérêt

4 la fête = a holiday / festival
la fête du village = the village fair
– In France, festivals are often associated with a religious day – une fête religieuse.

Le premier mai c'était la fête du village. Il y avait un marché et le soir on a pris un grand repas. On a bien mangé, on a dansé et on a chanté – c'était chouette, on s'est bien amusé.

fêter = to celebrate
un mariage = a wedding
une boum = a party
une pièce = a play
un concert = a concert
un spectacle = a show
un feu d'artifice = fireworks

5 Comment préfères-tu voyager?

Je préfère voyager	en avion en train en voiture en bus à vélo à pied	parce que	c'est rapide c'est confortable c'est pratique ce n'est pas cher c'est bon pour la santé

The word list on page 94 will help you expand on what you already know.

6 Il y a eu un accident de route. = There's been a road accident.
On est sur la nationale 12 près de ... = We're on the N12 near ...
Un homme / le conducteur a été blessé. = A man / the driver has been hurt.

Il faut une ambulance.	= An ambulance is needed.
Les voitures se sont percutées.	= The cars crashed into each other.
La voiture a heurté un arbre / un camion.	= The car crashed into a tree / a lorry.
La voiture est entrée en collision avec une moto.	= The car crashed into a motorbike.
La voiture roulait trop vite.	= The car was going too fast.
Le conducteur ne s'est pas arrêté.	= The driver didn't stop.
Le conducteur a essayé de doubler.	= The driver tried to overtake.
J'ai pris le numéro d'immatriculation.	= I took the registration number.
L'accident s'est produit à dix heures.	= The accident happened at 10 am.
Le conducteur n'a pas vu la moto.	= The driver didn't see the motorbike.
Le conducteur a démarré sans regarder.	= The driver started off without looking.
Il a brûlé les feux.	= He went through the lights.
Il y avait beaucoup de circulation.	= There was a lot of traffic.
C'était la faute du conducteur.	= It was the driver's fault.
un témoin	= a witness

Going for an A?

Faites une présentation de votre ville (sur cassette) pour un touriste français. Décrivez votre ville, les distractions et dites ce que vous pensez de votre ville.

- Remember, you should always try to give a reason for an opinion and link statements together using **parce que** – see Notes/Options 3 and 5 and learn the phrases. Use this cue card to express your opinions about the town where you live.

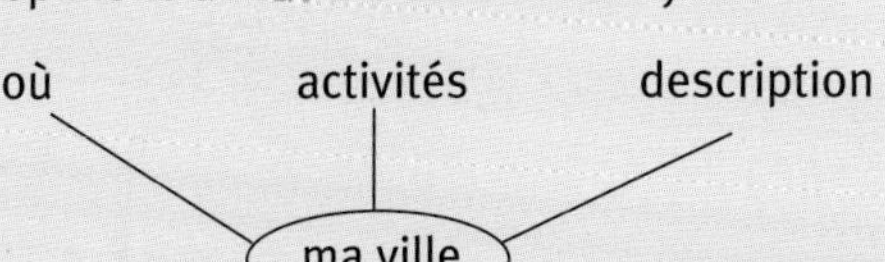

Test yourself

- At this level the examiners are looking for accuracy in written exercises and in particular the tenses. Task 1 concentrates on the present tense and Task 2 on the perfect and imperfect tenses. Make sure you are happy with these tasks; if you need help look at the grammar section.

Task 1 Writing

Où préférez-vous habiter? En ville ou à la campagne? Dans votre pays ou à l'étranger?

Ecrivez 120 mots. Donnez vos raisons.

Use both the Foundation and Higher Notes/Options to check your work.

Task 2 Writing

Vous avez vu un accident de route en ville hier soir. Décrivez ce qui s'est passé.
Ecrivez 150 mots.

- Remember to say where you were. For example: **J'étais dans la rue.** Also say what the weather was like; such as **Il pleuvait quand l'accident s'est produit.** (It was raining when the accident happened.)

Use phrases from the Notes/Options on page 44 (especially from 6) to help you.

Task 3 Reading

Lisez cet article.

Port-Vendres: la voiture a plongé par bêtise

Le spectaculaire plongeon d'une voiture, jeudi vers 19 heures, dans les eaux du port de Port-Vendres, n'était finalement pas dû à une fausse manoeuvre mais à une simple bêtise.

Une jeune femme de la région venait de garer son véhicule sur le quai de la Douane et était partie faire une course, oubliant de mettre le frein à main. Le temps de tourner le dos et l'auto a commencé à glisser avant de tomber dans l'eau sous le regard sidéré des passants.

Une foule a bien vu un homme remonter à la surface, avant l'arrivée de la propriétaire, mais ce dernier ne sortait pas du véhicule. Il s'agissait d'un sauveteur qui s'était immédiatement jeté dans le port au cas où de possibles occupants auraient besoin* d'aide.

De retour sur terre à la nage, c'est donc également lui qui a été réchauffé par les sapeurs-pompiers avant que les gendarmes ne recueillent son témoignage.

* *auraient besoin* = would need

Choisissez la bonne réponse, A, B ou C.

1 Qu'est-ce qui s'est passé, jeudi dernier à Port-Vendres?

A ☐ Une voiture est tombée dans l'eau.

B ☐ Une voiture a percuté une autre voiture.

C ☐ Une voiture a renversé un cycliste.

2 Pourquoi l'accident s'est-il produit?

A ☐ La conductrice a fait une fausse manoeuvre.

B ☐ La voiture avait glissé sur la chaussée.

C ☐ La conductrice a agi d'une façon distraite.

3 Qu'est-ce que la conductrice avait oublié?

A ☐ de faire une course.

B ☐ d'immobiliser la voiture.

C ☐ de klaxonner.

4 Qui était l'homme qui est remonté à la surface?

A ☐ un passager qui sortait de la voiture.

B ☐ le propriétaire du véhicule.

C ☐ un sauveteur.

5 Comment l'homme a-t-il regagné le quai?

A ☐ Sans l'aide de personne.

B ☐ Les sapeurs-pompiers l'ont aidé.

C ☐ Il a appelé les gendarmes à son aide.

Answers

TASK 3

1 A; 2 C; 3 B; 4 C; 5 A

For your own notes

Checklist

How do you feel about these?
In French, can you:

	Fine	Help!
Food shopping		
1 ask where shops are?	❑	❑
2 ask for opening times?	❑	❑
3 ask if they sell ...?	❑	❑
4 ask for items (by weight, quantity, containers)?	❑	❑
5 say that it is all you want?	❑	❑
6 pay for goods and check the change?	❑	❑
7 understand information about discounts, special offers, and so on?	❑	❑
Clothes shopping		
8 name the clothes?	❑	❑
9 give your size?	❑	❑
10 ask for particular colours and materials?	❑	❑
11 say you want an item, or why not, and pay?	❑	❑
12 give simple opinions?	❑	❑
At the post office		
13 ask where a post office is?	❑	❑
14 say where you want to send a letter, postcard or parcel? ask how long it will take? ask how much it costs? ask for stamps? ask if there is a telephone nearby?	❑	❑
15 ask for a phone card?	❑	❑
16 give your phone number?	❑	❑
17 ask to make a reverse charge call?	❑	❑
At the bank / bureau de change		
18 exchange money? check the exchange rate? ask for coins / notes of a certain type?	❑	❑

Going shopping

The word lists on pages 96–99 will point you in the right direction when you're in town.

Remember to think positive wherever possible; concentrate on the clothes you like most, or the food you most like to eat.

Once again, try to picture yourself in a French shopping centre with a list of things to do. Could you manage to get everything done?

Help is at hand!

		Notes/Options
1	Où est ...	= Where is ...
	la boucherie?	= the butcher's?
	la boulangerie?	= the baker's?
	le bureau de tabac?	= the tobacconist's?
	le centre commercial?	= the shopping centre?
	la charcuterie?	= the delicatessen (pork butcher's)?
	la confiserie?	= the sweet shop?
	l'épicerie?	= the grocer's?
	la pâtisserie?	= the cake shop?
	la pharmacie?	= the chemist's?
	la poissonnerie?	= the fishmonger's?
	la poste?	= the post office?
	le supermarché?	= the supermarket?

– *Beware!* **La librairie** *is the bookshop* *not* *the library!*

2	A quelle heure ferme le magasin?	= When does the shop close?
	Vous fermez à quelle heure?	= When do you close?
	Vous ouvrez à quelle heure?	= When do you open?
	A quelle heure ouvre le magasin?	= When does the shop open?

HEURES D'OUVERTURE	opening times
lun – ven	= Monday–Friday
de 8h 30 à 12h	de = from à = to
de 14h à 18h 30	14h = 2 pm 18h 30 = 6.30 pm
sam de 8h 30 à 17h 30	sam = Saturday 8.30 am – 5.30 pm

3	Avez-vous ...	= Do you have ...
	du pain?	= some bread?
	du fromage?	= some cheese?
	de l'eau?	= some water?
	des fraises?	= some strawberries?

On fait des achats – Foundation

Look at the foods on page 98. Then add six foods from pages 96–97 to the list on page 98: choose words you find hard to remember.

4 Asking for amounts of food

Je voudrais ...			
un demi-kilo	de	raisins	$\frac{1}{2}$ kilo
500 grammes		beurre	500 g
une livre		fraises	a pound
un kilo		bananes	a kilo
un morceau		fromage	a piece of
une portion		frites	a portion of
une tranche		jambon	a slice of
un paquet		thé	a packet of
une bouteille		coca	a bottle of
un litre		lait	a litre of
une boîte		haricots verts	a tin of
une douzaine	d'	oeufs	a dozen

Je suis désolé(e) il n'y a plus de poisson. = I'm sorry there's no more fish.

5 Et avec ça? = Is there anything else?

Non, c'est tout. = No, that's all.

Un peu plus. = A bit more.

Ça suffit. = That's enough.

Ça va très bien. = That's fine.

6 Les bananes sont à combien? = How much are the bananas?

Le melon coûte combien? = How much is the melon?

Les bananes sont à 1 € le kilo. = The bananas are 1 € a kilo.

Le melon – c'est 1 €20 la pièce. = The melons are 1 €20 each.

Je vous dois combien? = How much do I owe you?

Ça fait combien? = How much is it?

C'est combien?

Ça fait 3 €.

J'ai seulement un billet de 20 €. = I've only got a 20 € note.

Voici la monnaie. = Here's the change.

– Be careful! **La monnaie** *is change not money.*

7 L'argent = money

un billet = a banknote

la pièce = the coin

la monnaie = the change

soldes = sales

en promotion = on special offer

réduction = reduction

remise de 5% sur les livres = 5% off (discount) books

Going for a C?

A

2 derniers jours!
SOLDES
50% sur maillots de bains

B

Promotion
Fruits de la région
Melons 1 € la pièce*

C

Réductions pour les étudiants
Rayon Papeterie

Circle A, B or C.

1 Where can students get reduced prices on writing materials? A, B or C?

2 Where can you find fruit on special offer? A, B or C?

3 Where can you find half-price swimsuits in the sales? A, B or C?

* Here la pièce = each (not a coin!)

Answers

Going for a C?

1 = C, 2 = B, 3 = A.

8 See the word list on page 98 which is all about the clothes you might want to buy.

9 C'est quelle taille? = What size is it? (used for clothes)

Vous faites quelle pointure? = What shoe size are you?

Vêtements

30"	=	75 cm	=	soixante-quinze
32"	=	80 cm	=	quatre-vingts
34"	=	86 cm	=	quatre-vingt-six
36"	=	91 cm	=	quatre-vingt-onze
38"	=	97 cm	=	quatre-vingt-dix-sept
40"	=	102 cm	=	cent deux
42"	=	107 cm	=	cent sept
Size 8	=	36	=	trente-six
10	=	38	=	trente-huit
12	=	40	=	quarante
14	=	42	=	quarante-deux
16	=	44	=	quarante-quatre

Chaussures

2	=	35	=	trente-cinq
3	=	36	=	trente-six
4	=	37	=	trente-sept
5	=	38	=	trente-huit
6	=	39	=	trente-neuf
7	=	41	=	quarante et un
8	=	42	=	quarante-deux
9	=	43	=	quarante-trois
10	=	44	=	quarante-quatre

Je fais du 41. = I'm a size 41.
petit(e) = small
moyen(ne) = medium
grand(e) = large

Revise with the numbers on page 108.

10 Revise colours on page 79.

en coton = cotton
en soie = silk
en laine = wool
en nylon = nylon
en cuir = leather
en plastique = plastic

11 Vous acceptez les cartes de crédit? = Do you accept credit cards?

POSITIVE	
J'aime **la** robe.	= I like the dress.
Je **la** prends.	= I'll take it.
C'est à la mode.	= It's fashionable.
C'est cool!	= It's great!
Je préfère ...	= I prefer ...
J'aime **le** pullover!	= I like the jumper!
Je **le** prends.	= I'll take it.
J'aime **les** chaussures!	= I like the shoes!
Je **les** prends.	= I'll take them.

NEGATIVE	
Je n'aime pas la robe.	= I don't like the dress.
Je ne la prends pas, merci.	= I won't take it, thank you.
C'est démodé.	= It's unfashionable.
C'est trop cher.	= It's too expensive.
Je n'aime pas la couleur.	= I don't like the colour.
Je n'aime pas le pullover.	= I don't like the jumper.
Je ne le prends pas.	= I won't take it.
Je n'aime pas les chaussures.	= I don't like the shoes.
Je ne les prends pas.	= I won't take them.

12 Problèmes

Je peux l'essayer? = Can I try it on?

C'est trop long!

C'est trop court!

C'est trop cher!

C'est trop grand!

C'est trop petit!

Je n'aime pas la couleur!

On fait des achats – Foundation

13 A la poste	= At the post office
Où est la poste / le bureau de poste?	= Where is the post office?
Où est la boîte aux lettres?	= Where is the letter box?
pour aller à = où est	– La boîte à lettres *can also be used.*

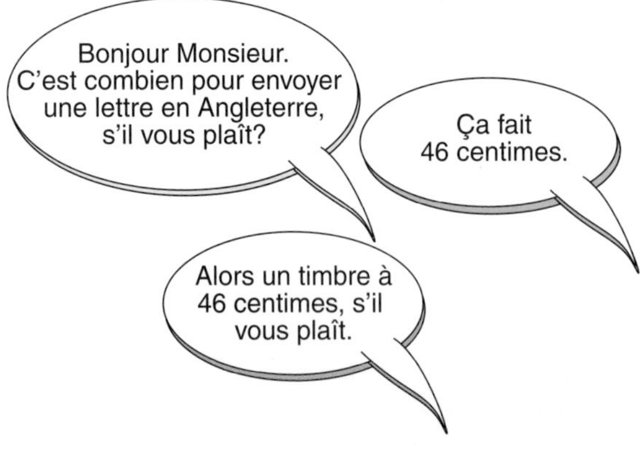

14 Je voudrais envoyer ...	= I would like to send ...
une lettre	= a letter
une carte postale	= a postcard
un timbre	= a stamp
un paquet	= a parcel
peser	= to weigh
Ça prendra combien de temps?	= How long will it take?
Trois ou quatre jours.	

Bonjour Madame. Je voudrais envoyer un paquet en Ecosse s'il vous plaît.

Il faut le peser – voilà ça fait trois euros Monsieur.

Ça prendra combien de temps?

Trois ou quatre jours. Il fait remplir cette fiche.

Est-ce qu'il y a une cabine téléphonique près d'ici?

Je voudrais un timbre pour l'Angleterre

A la poste

Ça prendra combien de temps / de jours?

Je voudrais envoyer un paquet. C'est pour envoyer un paquet.

Il fait remplir cette fiche.	= You'll have to fill in this form.
une cabine téléphonique	= a phone booth
Il y a un téléphone près d'ici?	= Is there a phone nearby?
15 Je voudrais une carte téléphonique s'il vous plaît.	= I'd like a phone card, please.

16 Mon numéro de téléphone c'est le 04-67-58-02-50.

– Remember – the French give phone numbers as 04, 67, 58, 02, 50 – in tens – **zéro quatre**, **soixante-sept**, **cinquante-huit**, **zéro deux**, **cinquante**. *Practise your own phone number in the same way.*

17 Je peux téléphoner en PCV?	= Can I make a reverse charge call?
18 Au bureau de change	= At the exchange bureau
Bonjour Madame, je voudrais changer de l'argent et des chèques de voyage.	= I'd like to change some money and some travellers cheques.
Dans quelle devise?	= In which currency?
la monnaie	= currency (also means change)
une livre sterling	= a pound sterling
Vous avez une pièce d'identité?	= Have you got any ID?
Oui, voici mon passeport.	= Here's my passport.
Le cours est à combien?	= What is the rate of exchange?
C'est à 1 euro 40 à la livre.	= It's at 1 euro 40 to the pound.
Il y a une commission?	= Is there a commission charge?
Je peux avoir des billets de 10 euros et des pièces de 1 euro?	= Could I have some 10 euro notes and some 1 euro coins?
Signez ici.	= Sign here.
Passez à la caisse.	= Go to the cash desk.

Test yourself

Shopping is another very popular examination topic especially in the speaking test and role play exercise. Be ready for an unexpected element signposted by a question mark or an exclamation mark in a box or **Répondez à la question** on your cue card.

When you are preparing for your role play exercises, think carefully about the situation and try to anticipate the unexpected element which will be a logical step in the situation. Think of all possible elements. Usually the unexpected will be a 'problem' such as there being no more of the item you want to buy so that you have to change your request. Or something might be the wrong size or colour, or too expensive. You might also have to give a simple opinion or preference.

Try to 'spot' the task during your preparation and listen carefully to the examiner. You might need to choose between two items so listen carefully so that you can make the choice and give a reason for your preference.

Here are some more role play exercises.

Task 1 **Speaking**

What would you say or ask for each of the items in these pictures?

Task 2 **Speaking**

A la poste

1 Say you want to send a letter to England.

2 Ask how much a stamp is.

3 Ask how long it will take.

4 Ask for 4 stamps.

Task 3 **Speaking**

Au magasin des chaussures

Examiner: Bonjour Monsieur / Mademoiselle. Vous désirez?

1 Candidate: (Demandez une paire de chaussures. Donnez la couleur.)

Examiner: Bon, des chaussures rouges / noires / bleues, etc. Quelle est votre pointure?

2 Candidate: (Répondez à la question.)

Examiner: Très bien. Voici une paire.

3 Candidate: (Demandez le prix.)

Examiner: Ça fait 50 euros.

4 Candidate: (Vous prenez les chaussures, que dites-vous?)

Examiner: Très bien. Alors passez à la caisse.

Task 4 **Speaking**

A la banque

Vous avez £50 (en billets de banque) et £100 en chèques de voyage.

Imaginez la conversation.
Ecrivez la conversation.

Check back to Notes/Options 18 and see how much you have got right.

Answers

TASK 1

1 Vous avez des bananes?
2 Je voudrais un kilo de bananes.
3 Je voudrais 500 grammes de fraises.
4 C'est combien?
5 J'ai seulement un billet de 20€.

TASK 2

1 Je voudrais envoyer une lettre en Angleterre.
2 Un timbre pour l'Angleterre - ça fait combien?
3 Ça / La lettre prendra combien de temps? Quand est-ce que la lettre arrivera? = When will the letter arrive?
4 Je voudrais quatre timbres s'il vous plaît.

TASK 3

1 Je voudrais des chaussures rouges / noires / bleues (etc).
2 Je fais du (+ size).
3 C'est combien?
4 Je les prends. Merci.

Checklist

How do you feel about these?
In French, can you:

		Fine	Help!
1	answer the Foundation Checklist on page 47?	❑	❑

If you've ticked the Help! box, go back to the Foundation Notes/Options and revise!

Clothes shopping

		Fine	Help!
2	state and explain preferences about clothes / fashion?	❑	❑
3	make a complaint in a shop, explain the problem and ask for a refund or replacement?	❑	❑
4	discuss general shopping habits?	❑	❑

At the post office / making a phone call

		Fine	Help!
5	explain to somebody how to make a phone call	❑	❑
6	make a phone call saying who you are and who you wish to speak to?	❑	❑
7	send a postal order or a telegram?	❑	❑
8	report the loss of an item (what you've lost, where and when)?	❑	❑

Going shopping

The word lists on pages 96–99 will point you in the right direction when you're shopping in town.

Remember to think positive wherever possible; concentrate on the clothes you like most, or the food you most like to eat.

Once again, try to picture yourself in a French shopping centre with a list of things to do. Could you manage to get everything done?

HELP IS AT HAND!

Notes/Options

1 Once you've looked back at the Foundation Checklist and you feel confident – carry on!

2 J'adore le look ...

branché = fashionable
décontracté = relaxed
classique = classical

Je préfère porter un jean / un sweat / les vêtements de marque.	un sweat = sweatshirt les vêtements de marque = brand-name clothes
Je n'aime pas porter l'uniforme scolaire.	= I don't like wearing school uniform.
Être à la mode, c'est très important.	= It's important to be fashionable.
Je n'aime pas m'habiller comme tout le monde.	= I don't like dressing like everybody else.
Pour moi, les vêtements sont très importants.	= I think clothes count a lot (are important).
On vous juge selon les vêtements que vous portez.	= People judge you according to what you wear.

3 Problèmes

General

Ça ne marche pas, c'est cassé.	= It doesn't work, it's broken.

Clothes

Il y a une tache.	= There's a stain.
Il manque un bouton.	= There's a button missing.
La fermeture à éclair est cassée.	= The zip is broken.
C'est déchiré.	= It's torn.
Vous pouvez me rembourser?	= Can you give me a refund?
Voici le reçu.	= Here is the receipt.
Pouvez-vous remplacer la robe / le pantalon?	= Can you replace the dress / trousers?
Pouvez-vous faire nettoyer le blouson?	= Can you have the jacket cleaned?
le nettoyage à sec	= dry cleaning

4 Où faites-vous vos provisions?

Be ready in an exam to describe your normal shopping habits (present tense).
See page 110 and page 127 for help with the present tense. Use a dictionary if you need it.

Je fais mes provisions au supermarché. J'y vais tous les samedis. J'achète de la viande, des légumes et des produits laitiers, et mes produits de ménage – par exemple, la lessive – aux grandes surfaces. Je fais aussi des achats près de chez moi – j'achète mon pain à la boulangerie, au coin de la rue. J'aime faire mes courses au supermarché – je n'ai pas beaucoup de temps et ça m'arrange de faire la plupart de mes provisions une fois par semaine. C'est plus pratique.

J'achète mes vêtements en ville. Je fréquente les grands magasins et les petites boutiques. J'achète, de temps en temps des vêtements de marque mais je trouve que, souvent, ça coûte trop cher! C'est bête de dépenser tellement d'argent sur un ou deux articles! J'adore faire du lèche-vitrines avec mes amis.

faire du lèche-vitrines	= to go window shopping

Remember you must be able to describe a recent shopping trip (perfect tense).

5 un appel téléphonique	= a phone call
décrochez	= pick up the receiver
introduisez une pièce	= put in a coin
attendez la tonalité	= wait for the tone
faites le code	= dial the code
composez le numéro	= dial the number

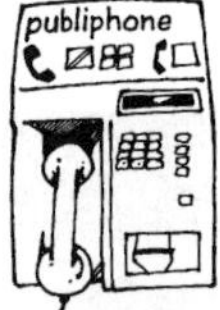

6 Je voudrais parler à / avec ...	= I'd like to speak to ...
C'est de la part de James Baker.	= It's James Baker calling.
Je peux lui laisser un message?	= Can I leave him / her a message?

When answering the phone in France, people say 'Allô' and don't tend to give the number as you would in England.

7 Je voudrais envoyer un mandat-postal / un télégramme en Angleterre.	un mandat postal = a postal order un télégramme = a telegram
8 Au bureau des objets trouvés	= At the lost property office
J'ai perdu mon portable.	= mobile phone
ma montre.	
mon sac.	
Quand?	
C'était hier.	
ce matin.	
il y a deux heures.	= two hours ago.
Où?	
Je l'ai perdu(e) dans le parc.	
dans le bus.	
en ville.	
Décrivez l'objet.	
C'est (+ couleur)	
C'est en coton / en laine / en cuir / en métal / en argent / en or.	argent = silver or = gold
C'est marqué à mon nom.	= My name is on it.
C'est de quelle marque?	= What make is it?
C'est un appareil Canon.	
une montre Swatch.	

For your own notes

....

....

....

....

....

....

....

....

Going for an A?

There is a lot of scope at this level to allow you to give your personal opinions and the reasons for your opinions. You should, however, not only be able to give facts and personal opinions, but also understand the opinions of others.

Learn the expressions Notes/Options 2 and all the new vocabulary.

Remember that most of the exam listening and reading questions will be in French, but there will be at least one exercise which will require answers in English. Remember, if the questions are in English answer in English.

When you are revising use a dictionary to help you with new words, but try to answer as many of the questions as you can before you look things up. No dictionaries are allowed in the exams!

Test yourself

Task 1 **Reading**

Read these letters sent in to a magazine. Answer Questions 1–4 in English and tick the correct box for number 5.

Je trouve que porter des vêtements de marque c'est nul. Ce n'est pas parce qu'on porte des trucs de marque qu'on se fait plus d'amis. Je n'ai rien de marque mais, en revanche j'ai plein d'amis - ils me trouvent sympa. Ce qui les intéresse, c'est mon caractère et non mes habits alors ... sois naturel et sympa avec tout le monde, c'est ça le secret du bien-être.

Charlotte, 15 ans, Perpignan

Bien sûr, il faut porter des vêtements de marque! Cela nous permet d'adopter un style, de montrer notre personnalité et de nous affirmer.

Les habits sans marque sont communs, et ceux qui les portent prouvent leur manque de goût. Mais chacun peut penser ce qu'il veut et certains de mes amis s'habillent sans marques.

Marie-Cécile, 16 ans, Besançon

1 According to Charlotte what can designer clothes not help you do?

2 Why does Charlotte think she has a lot of friends?

3 Why does Marie-Cécile think designer clothes are important (give two details)?

4 What does she think about people who don't wear designer clothes?

5 Marie-Cécile's last comment shows that:

- **a** all her friends wear designer clothes. ☐
- **b** all of her friends wear non-designer clothes. ☐
- **c** she does not notice what her friends wear. ☐
- **d** some of her friends wear designer clothes. ☐

Answers

TASK 1

1 Make friends.

2 They think she's nice / they are not bothered about what she wears, they are more interested in her character than her clothes.

3 Designer clothes let you adopt a certain style / show your personality / assert yourself (any 2 of 3).

4 They show a lack of taste.

5 (d).

Take a break

Now look back at the Checklist on page 53 – you should now be feeling fine for all of the questions.

For your own notes

Au café / Au restaurant – Foundation

Checklist

How do you feel about these?
In French, can you:

		Fine	Help!
1	express simple opinions about food?	❑	❑
2	accept / decline offers of food and drink?	❑	❑
3	ask for a table for yourself / a group of people?	❑	❑
4	say you have reserved a table?	❑	❑
5	attract the waiter's / waitress' attention?	❑	❑
6	ask for food and items on the table?	❑	❑
7	ask about availability of food and drink?	❑	❑
8	ask for the menu?	❑	❑
9	ask for a fixed price menu?	❑	❑
10	choose and order drinks, snacks, meals?	❑	❑
11	ask for an explanation of something on the menu?	❑	❑
12	ask for things missing from the table?	❑	❑
13	make a simple complaint?	❑	❑
14	express simple opinions about a meal?	❑	❑
15	ask for and settle the bill?	❑	❑

Going for a snack?

The word lists on pages 100–102 should give you plenty of ideas about what you need to know about this topic area. Everyone loves food in one way or another! Enjoy talking about your likes and dislikes! Be creative, and draw illustrated menus of your ideal meal, a healthy meal and an especially unhealthy one.

Help is at hand!

		Notes/Options
1	Tu aimes le fromage?	
	Oui, j'aime le fromage.	= Yes, I like cheese.
	J'aime beaucoup le fromage.	= I like cheese very much.
	J'adore le fromage.	= I love cheese.
	Mon plat préféré c'est ...	= My favourite dish is ...
	C'est très bon!	= It's good!
	C'était très bon!	= It was good! *– Always use* **bon** *for* **good** *when describing food or drink.*
	C'est délicieux!	
	C'était délicieux!	
	Tu aimes le poisson?	
	Je n'aime pas le poisson.	
	Je déteste le poisson.	
	Ce n'est pas bon!	
	Je ne mange pas de poisson.	= I don't eat fish.
	Ça me rend malade!	= It makes me feel ill!
2	Tu veux / Vous voulez du pain?	= Do you want some bread?
	Oui, je veux bien s'il te plaît / s'il vous plaît.	= Yes please, I'd like some.
	Tu veux / Vous voulez encore du pain?	= Do you want some more bread?
	Oui, je veux bien.	
	Oui, je voudrais encore du pain.	= Yes, I'd like some more bread.
	Je peux reprendre de la glace?	= Can I have some more ice-cream?
	Oui, bien sûr, sers-toi / servez-vous!	= Yes of course, help yourself.
	Tu veux / Vous voulez (encore) de la viande?	= Do you want some (more) meat?
	Oui, s'il te plaît / s'il vous plaît, j'ai faim!	= Yes please, I'm hungry!
	Merci – j'ai assez mangé.	= No thank you – I've eaten enough. *– Remember* **merci** *can mean* **no** *as well as* **thank you**.
		assez = enough

	Tu veux / Vous voulez encore de l'eau?	
	Merci, j'ai assez bu.	= I've had enough to drink.

3	Je voudrais une table pour trois personnes.	= I would like a table for 3.
4	J'ai réservé une table.	= I've reserved a table.
	C'est au nom de Woods.	= It's in the name of Woods. *– Be prepared to spell your name!*
5	Garçon!	= Waiter!
	S'il vous plaît Monsieur	= to the waiter
	Madame	= to the waitress
	Mademoiselle	= to a young waitress (of your age)
6	Tu peux / Vous pouvez me passer le beurre s'il te plaît / s'il vous plaît?	= Please would you pass me the butter? *– Remember* **vous** *is used to address older people and / or people you do not know well.*
	Tu me passes le sel s'il te plaît?	le sel = the salt
	Vous me passez le poivre s'il vous plaît?	le poivre = the pepper
7	Vous avez du poisson?	= Have you any fish?
	Vous avez des frites?	= Have you any chips?
	Vous avez des sandwichs au jambon?	= Have you any ham sandwiches?
8	Je peux avoir la carte s'il vous plaît?	la carte = the menu
	Je voudrais la carte des vins s'il vous plaît.	la carte des vins = the wine list
9	Je voudrais le menu à 15 euro.	= I'd like the 15 euro menu.
10	Qu'est-ce que vous prenez?	= What are you having?
	Je voudrais commander.	= I'd like to order.
	Je prends ...	= I'll have ...
	Je voudrais ...	= I'd like ...
	Comme entrée, je prends le pâté ...	= I'll have the pâté to start with ...
	et comme plat principal,	= as a main course
	je prends le poulet.	= I'll have the chicken.
	Et pour mon père, le poisson.	pour mon père = for my father
	Et vous désirez des légumes?	légumes = vegetables
	Oui, je voudrais des haricots verts et mon père voudrait des pommes vapeur.	= my father would like boiled potatoes
	Vous voulez un dessert?	dessert = dessert / sweet
	Oui, comme dessert ... une tarte aux pommes et une glace.	
	Qu'est-ce que vous prenez comme boissons?	= What would you like to drink?
	une boisson	= a drink
	Du vin, une bouteille de vin rouge.	

Remember the word lists on pages 100–102 to revise snacks, drinks and meals.

11	Le coq au vin, qu'est-ce que c'est?	= What is 'coq au vin'?
	C'est du poulet cuisiné dans une sauce avec du vin et des champignons – c'est bon!	
	cuisiné	= cooked
	préparé avec	= prepared with
12	Something's missing!	
	Garçon, il manque une fourchette!	= Waiter, there's a fork missing!
	un couteau	= a knife
	une cuillère	= a spoon
	Je n'ai pas de couteau.	= I haven't got a knife.
	Il n'y a pas de sel / de poivre / de sucre.	= There isn't any salt / pepper / sugar.
	Je voudrais de la moutarde.	= I'd like some mustard please.
13	Something's wrong!	
	Le potage est froid.	= The soup is cold.
	Le steak n'est pas assez cuit.	= The steak isn't cooked enough.
	cuit	= cooked
	Le poisson est trop cuit.	= The fish is too well done.
	J'ai commandé un steak à point / saignant.	
	à point	= medium
	saignant	= rare
	J'ai commandé mon repas il y a 40 minutes.	= I ordered my meal 40 minutes ago.
	J'attends depuis une heure!	= I've been waiting for an hour!

14 Vous avez bien mangé?	= Have you eaten well? / How was your meal?
C'était très bon / délicieux.	= It was very good / delicious.
On a bien mangé!	= We've eaten well.
J'ai bien mangé – merci!	= I've eaten well – thank you!
15 L'addition s'il vous plaît.	= The bill please.
Je voudrais l'addition / payer.	= I'd like the bill / to pay.
Le service est compris?	= Is the service included?
Les boissons sont comprises?	= Are the drinks included?
boissons en sus	= drinks extra *(often seen written on a menu)*
Vous acceptez les cartes de crédit?	= Do you accept credit cards?
Il y a une erreur dans l'addition.	= There's a mistake in the bill.
Je n'ai pas pris le poisson.	= I didn't have the fish.

Going for a C?

Learn all the vocabulary on pages 100–102.

Be prepared to talk about your likes and dislikes.

Give simple opinions about your favourite food.

- Remember talking about food can come up in other topics such as holidays – be ready to talk about the kind of food you ate in a different country. The French love to hear foreigners congratulating them on their cuisine.

En France j'ai mangé / j'ai pris ...

J'ai adoré la cuisine française! = I loved French cooking!

Test yourself

Try these role play exercises.

Task 1 **Speaking**

You are ordering a snack and drinks for yourself and a friend in a café.

1 Say you would like a hot drink (e.g. a white coffee).

2 Say you would like a cold drink (e.g. a lemonade).

3 Ask if there are any sandwiches.

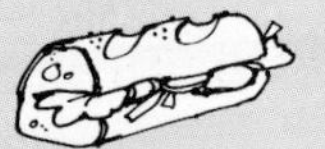

4 Ask for 2 sandwiches (e.g. cheese and ham).

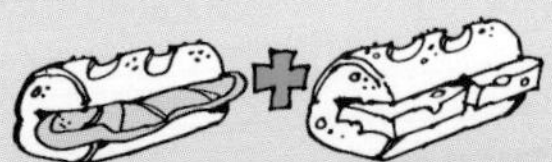

5 Ask how much it is.

Task 2 **Speaking**

Au restaurant

Bonsoir, je peux vous aider?

1 Say you would like a table for 2.

Où voulez-vous vous asseoir?

2 Say where you would like to sit.

Très bien. Voici le menu.
Que désirez-vous comme entrée?

3 Ask for 2 starters (e.g. soup and melon).

Bon. Et comme plat principal?

4 Ask if they have fish and ask if it is good.
Order the fish.

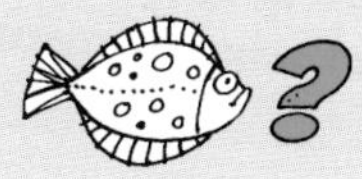

Oui, le poisson est très bon.

5 Ask where the toilets are.

Task 3 **Speaking**

Des problèmes au restaurant!

1 Say what you would like.

2 Say the soup is cold.

3 Say there is a spoon missing.

4 Ask for the salt.

Task 4 **Reading**

Lisez ce menu.

RESTAURANT CENTRAL

Les Entrées

Potage de légumes	3€50
Pâté maison	3€00
Melon	3€20

Les Plats

Steak grillé	10€00
Truite meunière	6€00
Coq au vin	6€00
Côtelettes de porc (sauce à la crème)	7€00
Omelette aux fines herbes	5€00

Les Légumes

Pommes vapeur	1€50
Haricots verts	3€00
Petits pois	2€50

Les Desserts

Plateau de fromages	3€00
Crème caramel	2€50
Glace (vanille/fraise)	3€00
Tarte aux pommes	3€50

Les Boissons

Vin rouge:	
Vin de pays de Murviel	4€00
Vin blanc:	
Château Cayan AOC	5€00
Jus de fruits	2€00
Eau minérale (Badoit)	2€50

Servis compris

C'est combien?

Exemple

= 3.50 €

1 = ... €

2 = ... €

3 = ... €

4 = ... €

5 = ... €

6 = ... €

7 = ... €

Task 5 **Listening**

Au restaurant

Listen to the CD (Chapter 8 Foundation). Play it twice.

Choisissez deux lettres pour chaque personne.

Exemple = B + E

1 ☐ + ☐

2 ☐ + ☐

3 ☐ + ☐

4 ☐ + ☐

Answers

TASK 1

1 Je voudrais un café-crème / un café au lait s'il vous plaît.

2 Je voudrais une limonade s'il vous plaît.

3 Avez-vous des sandwichs?

4 Je voudrais un sandwich au jambon et un sandwich au fromage.

5 C'est combien?

TASK 2

1 Je voudrais une table pour deux personnes.

2 Je voudrais une table près de la fenêtre. / Je voudrais m'asseoir à la terrasse.

3 Je voudrais le potage / le pâté / le melon, etc. (2 starters).

4 Vous avez du poisson? Le poisson est bon? Alors le poisson s'il vous plaît.

5 Il y a des toilettes? Où sont les toilettes s'il vous plaît?

TASK 3

1 Je voudrais du potage/de la soupe.

2 Le potage est froid.

3 Il n'y a pas de cuillère / Il manque une cuillère. (*une cuillère* can be spelt *une cuiller.*)

4 Je voudrais du sel s'il vous plaît.

TASK 4

1 = 3€20

2 = 6€

3 = 7€

4 = 2€50

5 = 3€50

6 = 4€

7 = 2€

TASK 5

1 M + K

2 D + L

3 A + N

4 F + H

Checklist

How do you feel about these?
In French, can you:

		Fine	Help!
1	answer the Foundation Checklist questions on page 56?	❑	❑

If you've ticked the Help! box, go back to the Foundation Notes/Options and revise.

		Fine	Help!
2	react to offers of food and drink and give your reasons?	❑	❑
	say how much more you want?	❑	❑
3	say how many there are in a group?	❑	❑
4	say where exactly you want to sit?	❑	❑
5	order a meal and change your order if something is not available?	❑	❑
6	make a complaint about a meal / the service?	❑	❑

Going for a snack?

The word lists on pages 100–102 should give you plenty of ideas about what you need to know about this topic area. Everyone loves food in one way or another! Enjoy talking about your likes and dislikes! List what you typically eat on a weekday and at weekends – three meals a day. Use a dictionary if necessary.

Help is at hand!

Notes/Options

1 Once you've looked back at the Foundation Checklist and you feel confident – carry on!

2 (See also Chapter 2 Higher Checklist 2 – page 15.)

Vous voulez encore du poisson?	
Je veux bien, c'est délicieux, j'ai très faim.	
Ça sent bon!	= It smells good!
Tu veux encore de la pizza? Merci, je ne l'aime pas trop – c'est un peu trop salé – je n'aime pas trop le goût.	= No thank you, I don't like it very much – it's too salty. I don't like the taste very much.
Tu veux encore de la tarte? Oui, je veux	
un peu	= a bit
un peu plus	= a bit more
la moitié de la tranche	= half of the slice
la moitié de la portion	= half of the portion
Ça suffit!	= That's enough!
J'en ai assez, merci.	= I've got enough thank you.

3 Vous êtes combien?

Nous sommes cinq.	= There are five of us.
On est cinq.	= There are five of us.

4 Où voulez-vous vous asseoir?

On voudrait s'asseoir près de la fenêtre.	= We'd like to sit near the window.
une table à la terrasse	= a table on the terrace
à l'intérieur	= inside

5

1a Que prenez-vous comme entrée Monsieur?

1b Je voudrais les hors-d'oeuvre s'il vous plaît.

2a Et comme plat principal?

2b Qu'est-ce que vous recommandez?

3a Le veau est très bon ce soir.

3b Bon alors le veau s'il vous plaît.

Qu'est-ce que vous recommandez?	= What do you recommend?
Il n'y a plus de veau!	= There's no more veal!
le plat du jour	= the dish of the day

1a Je regrette Monsieur il n'y a plus de veau.

1b Ah non – alors quel est le plat du jour?

2a Le plat du jour c'est le gigot – c'est délicieux!

2b Bon alors – je prends le gigot.

3a Merci Monsieur.

6 Encore des problèmes!

– See also Foundation Checklist 13, page 56.

Je n'ai pas commandé le poulet!	= I didn't order the chicken!
J'ai commandé il y a 30 minutes.	= I ordered 30 minutes ago.
J'attends depuis une heure!	= I've been waiting for an hour!
Mon verre / couteau / assiette / Ma fourchette } est sale.	= My glass / knife / plate / fork } is dirty.
On peut avoir du sel / du sucre?	= May we have some salt / sugar?
Voulez-vous changer l'assiette?	= Please change the plate.

For your own notes

....

....

....

....

....

....

....

....

....

....

....

....

....

Going for an A?

Remember to revise preferences about food and drink. You should also be able to understand the opinions of other people about food and drink.

Be prepared to talk about a recent trip you have made to a restaurant in France, elsewhere abroad or in the UK.

Food and drink, likes and dislikes could come up in conversations which include Daily Routine and Health and Fitness (attitudes to heathy and unhealthy eating habits) (see Chapters 1 and 2).

Test yourself

Task 1 **Speaking**

You have decided to celebrate your sister's 18th birthday. You telephone this restaurant to reserve a table.

Restaurant de la Place
Fêtez votre anniversaire!
Menu spécial – 15 €
(Gâteau compris!)

Allô, Restaurant de la Place, je peux vous aider.

1 Raison pour l'appel.

Alors, c'est pour quand?

2 Réservation – détails – date – heure.

C'est pour combien de personnes?

3 Répondez à la question.

C'est pour une fête spéciale?

4 Raison spéciale pour la fête.

Bon on va préparer un gâteau – comment s'appelle votre soeur? Comment s'écrit son prénom?

5 Épelez le prénom de votre soeur (pour le gâteau!).

Task 2 **Speaking**

The notes and pictures below give an outline of a day during a visit to your French friend's house last year. During your stay she celebrated her birthday.

Le matin

des cadeaux?

le petit déjeuner

La journée

réserver une table au restaurant

inviter les copains au restaurant

Les préparatifs

se changer – à quelle heure?

La fête

arrivée au restaurant

à quelle heure?

qu'avez-vous fait?

qu'avez-vous mangé?

Après la fête

le départ

vos impressions?

Now listen to the account on the CD (Chapter 8, Higher) to hear a model answer.

Task 3 **Reading**

Remplissez les blancs dans cette lettre.

Chère Juliette,

Salut! Merci de ton (1) .... d'anniversaire. Ça m'a fait plaisir – c'était chouette. J'ai (2) .... mon anniversaire avec mes copains, Marc, Anne et Olivier. On est (3) .... au restaurant italien – tu sais que j'adore la (4) .... italienne. Marc a dit qu'il avait (5) .... une table mais en arrivant il a (6) .... qu'il n'y avait pas de réservation! On a dû (7) .... une heure avant de manger – on avait (8) .... ! Finalement à 10 heures le serveur a apporté des pizzas mais on avait (9) .... des pâtes. Quel restaurant. On a bien rigolé – heureusement. En plus le serveur qui ne parlait pas un mot de français s'est trompé et l'(10) .... n'était pas correcte – c'était trop cher. Marc s'est mis en colère mais nous, on a bien rigolé. L'année prochaine je crois qu'on ira dans un restaurant français!

Answers

TASK 1

1 Je voudrais faire une réservation.
2 C'est pour (date + heure).
3 C'est pour (numéro) personnes.
4 On va fêter les 18 ans / l'anniversaire de ma soeur.
5 Ça s'écrit M-A-R-I-A

TASK 3

1 cadeau **2** fêté **3** allé/s **4** cuisine
5 réservé **6** vu/trouvé/découvert
7 attendre **8** faim
9 commandé **10** addition

For your own notes

....

Checklist

How do you feel about these?
In French, can you:

	Fine	Help!
1 give details about your school (size, type, buildings, facilities, number of pupils)?	❑	❑
2 ask for and give details about your school routine (timetable, class, homework, games)?	❑	❑
3 give a simple description of your school uniform?	❑	❑
4 say how you travel to and from school?	❑	❑
5 say which subjects you like / dislike and give simple reasons?	❑	❑
6 say which school clubs / teams you belong to?	❑	❑
7 give simple opinions about your school life?	❑	❑
8 say if you intend to leave or stay on at school?	❑	❑

Busy at school

The word lists on page 103 are about school, what you do there and school subjects. Learn the vocabulary.

Help is at hand!

	Notes/Options
1 Tu vas à quelle école?	
Mon collège s'appelle (+ name)	= 11–16 school
Mon lycée s'appelle (+ name)	= 11–18 school
Comment est ton collège?	
C'est un collège mixte.	
C'est petit / grand.	
un collège pour les garçons	
un collège pour les filles	
un collège catholique	
Comment sont les bâtiments?	
les bâtiments	= the buildings
Ils sont vieux / modernes.	= They are old / modern.
Il y a des préfabriqués.	= There are mobile classrooms.
Il y a des laboratoires	= laboratories
un laboratoire de langues	= a language laboratory
une salle d'informatique	= IT room
des terrains de sport	= sports pitches
une bibliothèque	= a library
un gymnase	= a gymnasium
un complexe sportif	= a sports centre / block
des courts de tennis	= tennis courts
une cour	= a courtyard
une cantine	= a dining room
	– *Be careful:* **un cours** *= a lesson!*
Il y a combien d'élèves?	
Il y a mille élèves.	= There are 1000 pupils.
Il y en a mille.	= There are 1000 (of them).
Il y a six cent cinquante élèves.	= There are 650 pupils.
2 Tu es en quelle classe?	
Je suis en seconde.	en seconde = Year 11
Comment est ton emploi du temps?	= What's your timetable like?
une matière	= a school subject
Tu as quelles matières le lundi?	
Le lundi j'ai ... (l') anglais de 9h à 10h.	= from 9 to 10 o'clock
... (le) français.	
... (les) sciences.	

The word list on page 103 will help you to revise school subjects.

A quelle heure commencent les cours?	= What time do lessons start?
Les cours commencent à neuf heures.	
A quelle heure finissent les cours?	= When do lessons finish?
Les cours finissent à quatre heures.	
Combien de temps dure un cours?	= How long does a lesson last?
Un cours dure 40 minutes / une heure.	= A lesson lasts 40 minutes / one hour.
La récréation est à quelle heure?	la récréation = break
La récréation est à 11 heures.	

Que fais-tu pendant la récréation? Je joue aux cartes, je prends un casse-croûte et je bavarde avec mes amis.	un casse-croûte = a snack je bavarde = I chat
A quelle heure prends-tu le déjeuner? Je prends le déjeuner à une heure à la cantine.	
As-tu beaucoup de devoirs? J'ai deux heures par / chaque soir.	= I have two hours per / each evening.
Oui, j'en ai trop!	= Yes, I have too much!
Tu fais du sport au collège? Oui, je joue au football, au tennis et je fais de la gymnastique.	

See page 85 for other sports vocabulary.

3 Tu portes un uniforme scolaire?

Oui je porte un pullover ? un pantalon ? / une jupe ? et une chemise ? .	Fill in the colours that you wear!

You can revise clothes vocabulary again by looking at page 98, and for colours look at page 79.

4 Comment viens-tu à l'école / au collège?	= How do you come to school?
Je viens à pied / à vélo / en voiture / en car.	en car = by bus / coach
5 Quelle matière préfères-tu? Pourquoi?	

POSITIVE	
Je préfère J'adore J'aime beaucoup	l'anglais le français les maths la biologie la géographie
C'est intéressant C'est facile C'est utile C'est amusant Je suis fort(e) en géo. J'aime le prof!	= interesting = easy = useful = funny = I'm good at geography. = I like the teacher!

NEGATIVE	
Je déteste Je n'aime pas du tout	le sport la technologie l'allemand les sciences
C'est ennuyeux C'est dur C'est difficile Je suis faible en maths. Je n'aime pas le prof!	= boring = hard = difficult = I'm poor at maths. = I don't like the teacher.

Quelle matière est-ce que tu n'aimes pas? Pourquoi pas?

6 Tu fais partie d'un club / d'une équipe scolaire?	= Do you belong to a school club / team?
Oui, je fais partie du	= Yes, I'm a member of the ...
club de drame	= drama club
club d'échecs	= chess club
club de photo	= photo club
Oui, je fais partie de l'équipe de rugby de tennis de netball	= Yes, I'm a member of the ... team.

7 Que penses-tu de ton collège?

POSITIVE	
Je l'aime!	J'ai beaucoup d'amis au collège. Les classes sont intéressantes. C'est un bon collège.
NEGATIVE	
Je ne l'aime pas!	Je n'ai pas beaucoup d'amis. C'est ennuyeux. C'est trop strict (too strict).

8 Qu'est-ce que tu vas faire après les examens? Tu quitteras l'école?	= What are you going to do after the exams? Will you leave school?
Je resterai à l'école pour passer mes 'A' levels.	= I'll stay at school to take my 'A' levels.
Je quitterai l'école.	= I'll leave school.
Ça dépend de mes résultats!	= It depends on my results!

Going for a C?

Add opinions about uniform, and subject, give simple reasons why.

Talk about what you did yesterday at school – use the following to help.

Hier	
j'ai fait	= I did / had
j'ai pris	= I took
j'ai travaillé	= I worked
j'ai mangé	= I ate
les classes ont commencé à	= lessons started at
je suis venu(e) au collège	= I came to school

Record Checklist questions 1 – 8 and leave a space on the cassette for your answer. Try not to look at the book!

Test yourself

Task 1 **Speaking**

Prepare a presentation about your school. Use this diagram to help.

mon collège
bâtiments – Il y a ...
matières – Je fais ... / J'aime ... / Je déteste ...
le sport – Je joue ...
clubs? équipes? – Je fais partie ...
uniforme – Je porte ...

Now record yourself. Play it back and see where you have had difficulty keeping going. Re-do that particular section.

Task 2 **Listening**

Listen to the CD (Chapter 9, Foundation). Play the track twice.

Complétez les notes en français et cochez (✓) la bonne case.

Le collège de Sophie

1. Collège: mixte ❑ pour des filles ❑
2. Combien d'élèves? ....
3. Bâtiments? vieux ❑ modernes ❑
4. Il y a **i** une cantine
   ii ....
   iii ....
   iv ....
5. Sophie préfère ....
   parce que ....
6. Les classes finissent à .... h. ....

Task 3 **Writing**

Write an article (100 words) about your school.

- Use the diagram for the speaking exercise (Task 1) to help!
- Check back to the answers 1–8 and correct the French if it is inaccurate.
- Ask a friend who is learning French to read it.

Give yourself a point for each item of information he / she understands. Aim for at least ten points.

- Try to put in your likes / dislikes and give a reason wherever possible.

Answers

TASK 2

1 mixte **2** 700 **3** modernes
4 **(i)** un gymnase; **(ii)** des laboratoires;
(iii) une bibliothèque
5 le français ..., le prof est sympa / amusant
6 4h 30.

Checklist

How do you feel about these?
In French, can you:

		Fine	Help!
1	**do the Foundation Checklist on page 66?**	❑	❑

If you've ticked the Help! box, go back and revise.

		Fine	Help!
2	**say how long you've been learning French – any other foreign languages you know?**	❑	❑
3	**talk about your timetable, terms and holidays?**	❑	❑
4	**discuss school subjects, rules, uniform?**	❑	❑
5	**say which exams you are taking and discuss your future plans at school?**	❑	❑
6	**describe special events / trips in the school year?**	❑	❑

Busy at school

The word lists on page 103 are all about school and what you do there, as well as the subjects that you learn. Learn the vocabulary.

Help is at hand!

Notes/Options

1 Once you've looked back at the Foundation Checklist and you feel confident – carry on!

2 Tu apprends le français / l'allemand / l'espagnol / l'italien / le russe depuis quand? — = German / Spanish / Italian / Russian
J'apprends le français depuis cinq ans. — = I have been learning French for five years.

3 Tu as combien de semaines de vacances scolaires?
On a deux semaines à Noël.
J'ai ... une semaine pour le mi-trimestre — = half term
deux semaines à Pâques — = Easter
une semaine en mai
six semaines en été
une semaine pour la Toussaint — *= the half term holiday in October*

Ça fait 13 semaines en tout.

C'est assez ou est-ce que tu voudrais des vacances plus longues comme en France? — assez = enough

Non, ça va. En France **on commence plus tôt** le matin et on finit plus tard le soir. En France on a **plus de vacances** mais pendant **le trimestre** scolaire il faut travailler dur et on travaille aussi le samedi matin – **je n'aimerais pas faire ça. Si les vacances sont trop longues on s'ennuie!** — = people start earlier; = more holidays; = the term; = I wouldn't like to do that. If the holidays are too long you get bored.

Et comment est ton emploi du temps?

C'est chargé mais assez bien équilibré. Je fais dix matières. Certaines matières sont obligatoires mais on peut aussi choisir certaines matières – il y a des options. — chargé = full; équilibré = balanced; obligatoire = compulsory; une option = an option

Be prepared to discuss what you do on your favourite / least favourite day, and say why you like / dislike that day.

4 See Foundation Notes/Options 5 and learn the following reasons for liking / disliking subjects / school / uniform.
Use a dictionary to check vocabulary if necessary.

Les matières

POSITIVE ☺ $\frac{18}{20}$	NEGATIVE ☹ $\frac{2}{20}$
Je reçois de bonnes notes.	Je reçois de mauvaises notes.
Je suis fort(e) en maths.	Je suis faible en maths.
Je trouve le travail facile.	Je trouve le travail difficile.
On s'amuse en classe.	On s'ennuie en classe.
Le prof est sympa – il explique bien la matière.	Le prof est nul – il n'explique pas bien la matière.

La discipline POSITIVE ✔	NEGATIVE ✘
Les profs sont assez stricts mais pas trop.	Les profs ne sont pas assez stricts. Les profs sont trop stricts.
Il y a une bonne ambiance.	Il y a une mauvaise ambiance.
Il n'y a pas trop de bruit.	Il y a trop de bruit.
On peut se concentrer.	On ne peut pas se concentrer.
On s'entend bien avec les profs et les élèves se respectent.	On ne s'entend pas bien avec les profs. Les profs et les élèves ne s'entendent pas bien.

L'uniforme POUR ✔	CONTRE ✘
Le matin, je sais quoi mettre.	Le matin je préfère m'habiller d'une façon différente de mes ami(e)s.
On ne voit pas la différence entre les élèves.	Il faut développer un style personnel.
Porter un uniforme, c'est bien pour la discipline!	
C'est cher au début, mais après, on dépense moins d'argent.	C'est trop cher – acheter un uniforme et d'autres vêtements!
C'est pratique!	Je déteste la couleur – c'est démodé.

5 Tu passes quels examens cet été?

Je passe des examens, des GCSE en français, en maths ...	je passe = I'm taking
les examens blancs	= 'mocks' / practice exams
J'espère réussir à mes examens.	= I hope to pass my exams.
rater un examen	= to fail an exam
Si je réussis à mes examens je vais continuer à faire des études.	= If I pass my exams I'm going to carry on with my studies.
Je voudrais passer mes 'A' levels – mon baccalauréat.	le bac = le baccalauréat
Je vais quitter le collège et je voudrais trouver un emploi.	= I'm going to leave school and I'd like to get a job.

6 Pendant l'année scolaire il y a

des pièces / des spectacles / des répétitions	= plays / entertainment / rehearsals
des soirées musicales	= musical evenings
une journée de compétitions sportives	= sports day
des réunions pour les parents et les profs	= parents' evenings
des conseils de classe	= staff meetings (to discuss individual class members)
des matchs de foot / tennis	= football / tennis matches
des voyages scolaires	= school trips
des échanges scolaires	= school exchange trips
une distribution des prix	= Speech Day / Prizegiving

Going for an A?

Be prepared to talk about what **normally** happens at the events in Checklist 6: D'habitude + present tense, on va, on voit, on reçoit, on donne, on regarde.

Be prepared to talk about events last year (perfect + imperfect tenses): L'année dernière, j'ai joué dans une pièce. J'ai joué le rôle de ... C'était chouette.

Be prepared to talk about school life in France as well as your own experience.

Remember: plus ... que = more than
moins ... que = less than

En France la journée scolaire est plus longue mais les vacances sont plus longues.

Test yourself

Task 1 **Reading**

La vie en terminale

Lisez le texte et remplissez les blancs.
David – élève

Dès la rentrée les profs n'ont qu'un mot à la bouche – le bac et encore le bac. Ça finit par devenir [L] (Exemple). On commence la philosophie – c'est une [1][ ] matière – il faut apprendre une méthodologie, c'est dur.

On a eu un [2][ ] blanc – le bac blanc – juste avant les vacances de février. Toutes les matières ont été écrites dans les [3][ ] de l'examen. C'était [4][ ] car cela m'a permis de voir ce que les profs attendaient de moi. Et on est [5][ ] stressé en juin.

J'ai commencé à [6][ ] en mai un petit peu tous les [7][ ]. En juin je m'y suis mis plus [8][ ].

Ecrivez dans la case la lettre du mot qui correspond

A = ancienne	**G** = jours
B = conditions	**H** = moins
C = difficile	**I** = nouvelle
D = examen	**J** = réviser
E = indispensable	**K** = sérieusement
F = inutile	**L** = ~~stressant~~ (exemple)

Task 2 **Reading**

Read the text and answer the questions in English.

Madame Panis – Professeur

La rentrée c'est le temps des bonnes résolutions. Elles peuvent se résumer en trois: bien suivre en classe (c'est le début de la mémorisation); reprendre ses notes pour les remettre en ordre; enfin continuer à mener une vie normale – à jouer au basket ou de la guitare si cela vous détend.

S'évaluer c'est l'un des objectifs du bac blanc. Si la surprise est agréable cela vous soulage; si elle ne l'est pas on a le temps de faire face au problème. Participer à un bac blanc c'est mettre 30% de chances en plus de son côté.

Le bac arrive toujours trop vite. Pour éviter d'être débordé au dernier moment mieux vaut s'y prendre le plus tôt possible. L'idéal serait d'avoir terminé vos révisions en juin pour tester vos connaissances à deux ou à l'aide d'exercices.

1 What, according to Madame Panis are the three resolutions to make at the beginning of the school year?

i ....

ii ....

iii ....

2 If students get a good mock exam result how do they feel?

3 Why, according to Madame Panis, is it a good idea to do a mock exam?

4 What should you do to avoid being swamped with work at the last minute?

5 How does she recommend revising?

Task 3 **Writing**

Ecrivez une liste des aspects positifs et négatifs dans votre collège.

POSITIVE	NEGATIVE
Les profs sont sympa. J'ai beaucoup de copains de classe.	Je n'aime pas l'uniforme – c'est démodé.

Use the Notes/Options to help! Try to write at least five positive and five negative things. Say what you would change if you could, e.g. Si je pouvais changer quelque chose, je ne porterais pas d'uniforme.

You might need to revise the conditional tense again here, so look at page 131.

Make sure you can do the Foundation speaking task on page 68.

Make a spider diagram which includes Avantages (positive) et Inconvénients (negative). (For help see page 70.)

Answers

TASK 1

1 I **2** D **3** B **4** E **5** H **6** J **7** G **8** K

TASK 2

1. i follow carefully/well in class; **ii** look back over class notes/keep class notes in order; **iii** carry on leading a normal life

2 relieved **3** It increases your chances of passing by 30%. **4** Start working as soon as possible. **5** With a friend (in a pair) and doing exercises

Checklist

How do you feel about these?
In French, can you:

	Fine	Help!
Work		
1 give information about future work plans?	❑	❑
2 give information about how you get to work and how long it takes?	❑	❑
3 say that somebody is out of work?	❑	❑
4 understand details about jobs, weekend jobs and work experiences?	❑	❑
5 say if you have a spare-time job and give details about it (hours, pay)?	❑	❑
6 give simple opinions about jobs?	❑	❑
7 say which jobs you and your family do?	❑	❑
Publicity		
8 understand and give simple opinions about adverts?	❑	❑
Communication		
9 ask and give a phone number and answer a phone call, saying who you are?	❑	❑
10 ask to speak to someone and take or leave a message?	❑	❑

Back to work

Make sure that you match up the checklist areas where you still need some help with the correct Notes/Options below. By now, you must be familiar with making the most of the word lists. Have a look at page 104. These are particularly useful to give you ideas about what you might do in the future.

Help is at hand!

	Notes/Options
1 Qu'est-ce que tu veux faire dans la vie?	= What job do you want to do?
Je veux être infirmière.	= I want to be a nurse.
J'espère être ingénieur.	= I hope to be an engineer.

See the word list on page 104.

Je veux travailler dans l'informatique.	= I want to work / a job in computers.
dans le commerce.	= in business.
dans un bureau.	= in an office.
avec le public.	= with the public.
dans l'industrie.	= in industry.
Je veux un métier intéressant.	= I want an interesting job.
un métier	= a job / profession
Je veux continuer avec mes études.	= I want to carry on studying.
Je veux aller en faculté / à l'université.	= I want to go to university.
Je veux trouver un emploi.	= I want to find a job.
Je veux faire un stage de formation.	= I want to do a training course.
Je veux faire un apprentissage.	= I want to do an apprenticeship.
Je veux faire un stage d'informatique.	= I want to do a computing course.
Je ne sais pas – je n'ai pas encore décidé ...	= I don't know – I haven't decided yet ...
ça dépend de mes résultats.	= it depends on my results.

Think about your future plans. Make sure you can say what you want to do – don't be surprised on the day of the exam!

2 Comment vas-tu au travail?	
J'y vais en bus / à pied / en train.	= I go by bus / on foot / by train.
Le trajet dure vingt minutes.	= The journey takes 20 minutes.
3 Ton père / ta mère / ton frère / ta soeur travaille?	= Does your father / mother / brother / sister work?
Oui il / elle est (+ job).	
Non il / elle est au chômage.	au chômage = unemployed
Il est chômeur.	= He is unemployed.
Elle est chômeuse.	= She is unemployed.

4 Les heures de travail sont de 9h à 5h. = The working hours are from 9–5 o'clock.

un travail à plein temps	= a full time job
un travail à mi-temps	= a part time job
on recherche vendeur	= wanted – a salesman
expérience essentielle	= experience is essential
un bon salaire	= good salary
C'est bien payé.	= It's well paid.
faire un stage	= to do work experience
J'ai fait un stage.	= I did my work experience.
{ chez (+ name of firm) dans un bureau dans une usine	{ at (+ firm) in an office in a factory
J'ai fait un stage de deux semaines.	= I did two weeks' work experience.
un emploi un boulot (slang)	= un travail = a job

5

Tu as un travail? Tu travailles? }	= Do you have a job?
Oui je travaille ... dans un supermarché. dans un magasin. dans un café. chez (+ name of firm). chez un coiffeur.	= Yes I work ... in a supermarket. in a shop. in a café. at (+ firm). at a hairdresser's.
Oui, je distribue des journaux. je fais du babysitting.	= Yes, I deliver papers. = I babysit.
Non, je n'ai pas de travail.	= No, I haven't got a job.
Je travaille le samedi / tous les soirs / deux soirs par semaine.	= I work on Saturdays / every evening / two evenings a week.
C'est bien payé? Oui, pas mal ... je reçois 3 livres de l'heure. je gagne 20 livres par jour.	= Is it well paid? = Yes it's not bad ... – I get £3 an hour. – I earn £20 a day.
Non c'est mal payé/Ce n'est pas bien payé.	= No it's badly paid / It isn't well paid.
Avec l'argent ... je fais des achats. je fais des économies.	= With the money ... = I buy things. = I save up.
Que penses-tu de ton travail?	

POSITIVE ☺	NEGATIVE ☹
C'est intéressant. C'est bien payé. J'aime travailler avec le public.	C'est ennuyeux. C'est mal payé. C'est fatigant.

6 See the word list on page 104.

7 La Publicité: Advertising – useful vocabulary and phrases.

une annonce	= an advert
à mon avis	= in my opinion
la mode	= fashion
une photo	= a photo
une réclame	= an advert
un spot publicitaire	= a TV advert
J'aime la publicité à la télé ... ... c'est amusant.	= I like TV advertising = it's funny.
Je déteste la publicité à la télévision ... ... c'est bête ... ça ne représente pas la réalité	 = it's stupid = it doesn't represent reality

8/9 See Chapter 7 Foundation Checklist 16 – how to give a phone number.

Allô, **Nicola King** à l'appareil.	= Hello, it's Nicola King speaking. (When answering a call at home.)
Société Smith, Bonjour ...	= Smiths, Good morning ... (At work)

See also Chapter 7 Higher Checklist 6 – leaving a message.

Vous voulez laisser un message?	= Do you want to leave a message?
Oui, c'est de la part de Chris Woods. Non, je peux rappeler dans une demi-heure?	= Yes, it's Chris Woods speaking. = Can I ring back in half an hour?
Vous pouvez rappeler ... Ne quittez pas. Je vous passe à ...	= You can ring back ... = Hold on a moment. = I'm putting you through to ...
Vous pouvez me donner vos coordonnées?	= Can you give me your details (name and number)?

Going for a C?

Remember to give opinions about your choice of job!

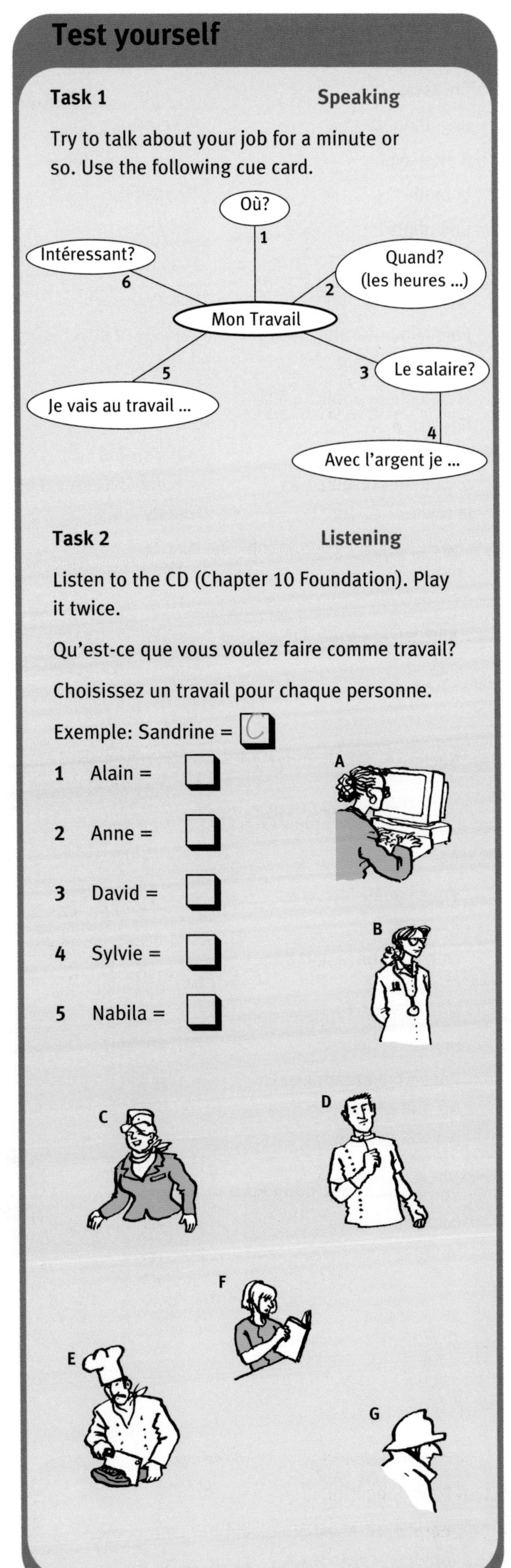

Test yourself

Task 1 **Speaking**

Try to talk about your job for a minute or so. Use the following cue card.

Task 2 **Listening**

Listen to the CD (Chapter 10 Foundation). Play it twice.

Qu'est-ce que vous voulez faire comme travail?

Choisissez un travail pour chaque personne.

Exemple: Sandrine = C

1 Alain = ☐

2 Anne = ☐

3 David = ☐

4 Sylvie = ☐

5 Nabila = ☐

Answers

TASK 2

1 = E 2 = B 3 = G 4 = F 5 = A

For your own notes

Checklist

How do you feel about these?
In French, can you:

	Fine	Help!
1 do the Foundation Checklist on page 72?	❑	❑

If you've ticked the Help! box, go back and revise.

	Fine	Help!
2 give reasons for your choice of study or job?	❑	❑
3 express hopes about your future plans after studying?	❑	❑
4 give details about jobs, weekend jobs and work experience?	❑	❑
5 understand and give opinions about different jobs?	❑	❑
6 make arrangements to be contacted by fax or phone?	❑	❑
7 ask what work others do?	❑	❑
8 enquire about the availability of work?	❑	❑

Back to work

Make sure that you match up the checklist areas where you still need some help with the correct Notes/Options below. By now, you must be familiar with making the most of the word lists. Have a look at page 104. These are particularly useful to give you ideas about what you might do in the future.

HELP IS AT HAND!

Notes/Options

1 Once you've looked back at the Foundation Checklist and you feel confident – carry on!

2/3

Que voudrais-tu faire dans la vie? Pourquoi?	
Je voudrais faire un stage. / continuer avec mes études.	
parce que / parce qu'	
Je dois réussir à mes études pour devenir avocat.	réussir = to be successful / to pass
aller en faculté	= to go to university.
Il faut faire des études supérieures pour être médecin.	= You have to do further studies to be a doctor.
On réussit avec des diplômes.	= You'll succeed with qualifications.
Les études sont indispensables.	= Studies are essential.
Je voudrais faire un stage, il faut une formation spécialisée pour travailler dans le tourisme.	= You have to have special training to work in tourism.
J'espère devenir professeur.	*– Do not put the* **un** *in!*

4 See the Foundation Checklist 4. You should be able to talk and write about the details as well as understand.

5 Des opinions sur les métiers – use a dictionary to check vocabulary you are not sure of.

Avantages – POSITIVE	Inconvénients – NEGATIVE
C'est bien payé / rémuneré.	C'est mal payé / rémuneré.
C'est un métier stimulant. / intéressant. / passionnant.	C'est un métier ennuyeux. / sans intérêt.
On peut voir le monde.	C'est fatigant.
On pourrait (= might / would be able to) vivre / voyager à l'étranger.	On doit travailler dans un bureau.
	Les heures sont longues.
Il y a des possibilités de promotion.	C'est un travail répétitif.
C'est un métier utile – ça rend service au public.	C'est un emploi sans avenir.
	C'est un métier peu assuré. (= not very secure)

Going for an A?

Faites correspondre les métiers (1–9) aux phrases A – I. Exemple 1 = D

Métiers	Phrases
– Je voudrais être / devenir ...	parce que ...
1 instituteur / institutrice	A je veux aider les gens
2 comptable	B l'actualité m'intéresse
3 informaticien / informaticienne	C je veux travailler en plein air
4 médecin	D j'adore les enfants
5 vétérinaire	E je voudrais travailler à l'étranger et parler des langues
6 journaliste	F les chiffres m'intéressent
7 jardinier / jardinière	G je veux gagner beaucoup d'argent
8 interprète	H l'informatique me passionne
9 président-directeur général (PDG) (managing director)	I je veux soigner les animaux

Answers

Going for an A?

2 F 3 H 4 A 5 I 6 B 7 C 8 E 9 G

6 Je voudrais envoyer un fax / envoyer un document par fax.	I'd like to send a fax / fax this document.
A l'attention de ...	= For the attention of ...
Mon numéro de fax est ...	= My fax number is ...
Vous pouvez me joindre à ...	= You can reach / contact me on / at (plus phone number or place).
Mon poste de téléphone est ...	= My extension is ...
Répondez-moi par fax / e-mail.	= Fax / e-mail me a reply.
Laissez un message sur le répondeur.	= Leave a message on the answerphone.
7 Que faites-vous dans la vie?	*– used for somebody you do not know well* = What's your job?
Quel métier exercez-vous / faites-vous?	= What is your profession?
8 Je vous écris pour demander si vous cherchez ...	I'm writing to ask if you need ...
un vendeur / une vendeuse	= shop assistant.
un serveur / une serveuse	= a waiter / waitress.
un moniteur / une monitrice	= an attendant.
en été.	= in the summer.
s'il y aura un travail temporaire	= if there will be any temporary work
J'ai lu dans le journal que vous cherchez ...	= I read in the paper that you are looking for ...
En réponse à votre annonce ...	= In reply to your advertisement ...
J'aimerais beaucoup travailler... en France. avec les enfants. dans un café.	
J'ai déjà travaillé comme ...	I've already worked as ...
Je suis très intéressé(e) par ce poste.	= This post appeals to me.
Je me permets de vous offrir mes services.	= I should like to apply for this post.
Je suis libre du **5 juillet** au **2 septembre**.	= I'm free from 5th July until 2nd September.
Je vous envoie mon CV.	= I enclose my CV.

Formal signing off:
Espérant que vous prendrez ma demande en considération je vous prie d'agréer, Monsieur / Madame, l'expression de mes sentiments les meilleurs.

Going for an A?

- Be prepared to explain what work experience you have had. Always have a reason why you would be good at this kind of job.
- Be ready to give details about your education, exams, which languages you speak and since when (Chapter 9 Higher Checklist 2).

Test yourself

Task 1 **Writing**

> **HÔTEL CENTRAL**
> Recherche serveur/serveuse
> juillet – août
> anglais indispensable!

Ecrivez une lettre au propriétaire de l'hôtel pour poser votre candidature à ce poste.

"Monsieur,

En réponse à votre annonce, je me permets ..."

Task 2 **Speaking**

You decide to ring up the Central Hotel. You have worked in a hotel as a waiter / waitress and want to work in France this summer. You phone the owner.

Hôtel Central Bonjour.

1 Saluez le / la propriétaire et expliquez pourquoi vous téléphonez.

Ah vous êtes anglais(e)! Depuis quand parlez-vous le français?

2 Répondez à la question.

Et vous avez de l'expérience dans l'hôtellerie?

3 Expliquez quand et où vous avez travaillé.

Et pourquoi est-ce que ce poste vous intéresse? Quand êtes-vous libre?

4 Expliquez pourquoi vous voulez travailler à l'Hôtel Central. Quand êtes-vous libre?

Bon. Envoyez-moi votre CV et je vais vous rappeler. D'accord?

Task 3 **Writing**

Ecrivez une lettre à une colonie de vacances pour demander s'il y aura du travail temporaire en été.

Remember do not use **Cher** / **Chère** in formal letters.

Remember to sign off properly.

Put in all relevant details about your experience.

Say why you want this job.

Check back to Notes/Options 8.

See the mock exam (Higher – page 123) for further reading practice related to work.

Answers

TASK 2

Bonjour Monsieur ... je m'appelle ...

1 Je vous téléphone au sujet de l'annonce. J'ai vu que vous demandez un serveur / une serveuse.

2 J'apprends le français depuis cinq ans.

3 Oui, j'ai travaillé comme serveur / serveuse l'année dernière, en été, dans un hôtel en Angleterre.

4 Je voudrais beaucoup travailler en France et j'aime travailler avec le public. Je suis libre du 1er juillet au 31 août. Merci Monsieur. Au revoir.

Take a break

If you have been working through the chapters in order from 1–10 – well done! You're nearly finished and ready for your exam. Why not now have a go at the mock exam (Chapter 12)?

Or you could look at the summary on page 78 and see if there are any areas where you still want to build your confidence.

As a recap, why not trawl through the word lists again and note any ten phrases you've forgotten. Write them and learn them.

For that extra confidence, and those extra marks, have a look at the international world vocabulary on pages 105–107.

Summary

My revision checklist

All about me
- Family ☐
- Pets ☐
- At the chemist's ☐
- Aches and pains ☐

General
- Numbers ☐
- Days, months, seasons ☐
- Telling the time ☐

At home
- My house ☐
- Household chores ☐

In town
- Places in town ☐
- Asking the way ☐
- Shopping for food ☐
- Eating out ☐
- Clothes and colours ☐

Free time
- TV & films ☐
- Where I go ☐
- What I did last weekend ☐
- What I'm going to do next weekend ☐

Work and school
- School subjects ☐
- My school ☐
- Jobs ☐
- My plans for after school ☐
- The international world ☐

Grammar
- The present tense ☐
- The past tense ☐
- The future tense ☐

On holiday
- Hotel ☐
- Camp site ☐
- Youth hostel ☐
- Countries ☐
- Nationalities ☐
- Weather ☐
- What I do ☐

Chapter 1 Moi

Les animaux	Animals
j'ai ... un chat ... un cheval ... un chien ... un hamster ... un lapin ... un oiseau ... un poisson rouge ... un serpent j'ai ... une araignée ... une souris	I have ... a cat ... a horse ... a dog ... a hamster ... a rabbit ... a bird ... a goldfish ... a snake I have ... a spider ... a mouse

Les couleurs		Colours
masculin	*féminin*	
blanc	blanche	white
bleu	bleue	blue
brun	brune	brown
gris	grise	grey
jaune	jaune	yellow
marron	marron	brown
noir	noire	black
orange	orange	orange
rose	rose	pink
rouge	rouge	red
vert	verte	green
violet	violette	violet, purple

La famille		Family
moi		me
mon frère	... aîné	my older brother
	... cadet	my younger brother
	... jumeau	my twin brother
mon père		my father
mon oncle		my uncle
mon cousin		my (male) cousin
mon grand-père		my grandfather
ma sœur	... aînée	my older sister
	... cadette	my younger sister
	... jumelle	my twin sister
ma mère		my mother
ma tante		my aunt
ma cousine		my (female) cousin
ma grand-mère		my grandmother
mes grands-parents		my grandparents

le bébé	baby
la nièce	niece
le neveu	nephew
mes parents sont divorcés / séparés	my parents are divorced / separated
mon oncle est célibataire	my uncle is single
j'ai un demi-frère / demi-soeur	I have a step-brother / step-sister

Chapter 1 Moi

Ça va?	How are you?
j'ai mal ... au bras ... au doigt ... au dos ... à l'estomac ... au genou ... au nez ... au pied ... au ventre	my arm hurts my finger hurts my back hurts / I've got backache I've got a stomach-ache my knee hurts my nose hurts my foot hurts my tummy hurts / I've got stomach-ache

j'ai mal ... à la cheville ... à l'épaule ... à la gorge ... à la jambe ... à la main ... à l'oreille ... à la tête	my ankle hurts my shoulder hurts I've got a sore throat my leg hurts my hand hurts my ear hurts / I've got earache my head hurts / I've got a headache

j'ai mal ... aux dents ... aux yeux	my teeth hurt / I've got toothache my eyes hurt

je me suis cassé le bras	I've broken my arm
je me suis coupé le doigt	I've cut my finger
je suis enrhumé(e)	I've got a cold
j'ai la grippe	I've got flu
j'ai de la fièvre	I've got a temperature
j'ai un coup de soleil	I'm sunburnt
je tousse	I'm coughing
je n'ai pas d'appétit	I've lost my appetite
j'ai mal au cœur	I feel sick
je suis malade depuis hier	I've been ill since yesterday
j'ai chaud / froid	I'm hot / cold

Chapter 1 Moi

À la pharmacie	At the chemist's
je voudrais ... un pansement ... un tube de crème antiseptique ... un tube de crème solaire je voudrais ... une brosse à dents ... une ordonnance je voudrais ... des comprimés ... des pastilles pour la gorge je voudrais ... du savon ... du shampooing ... du sirop ... du sparadrap je voudrais ... de l'aspirine ... de la crème antiseptique ... de la crème solaire	I'd like ... a bandage ... a tube of antiseptic cream ... a tube of sun cream I'd like ... a toothbrush ... a prescription I'd like ... some tablets ... some throat pastilles I'd like ... some soap ... some shampoo ... some cough mixture ... a plaster I'd like ... some aspirin ... some antiseptic cream ... some sun cream

je voudrais un médicament contre les maux de tête	I'd like some medicine for headaches
il faut appeler le médecin	you / one should call the doctor
quel est le dosage?	what is the dose?
prendre un comprimé le matin et le soir	take one tablet in the morning and in the evening
prendre une cuillerée avant les repas	take one spoonful before meals
nettoyer la plaie	clean the wound
mettre de la crème	apply some cream
rester au lit / garder le lit	stay in bed
ne bougez pas!	don't move!

Chapter 2 Chez moi

À la maison	At home
je dois... faire le repassage faire la cuisine faire la lessive faire la vaisselle je dois... faire du babysitting faire du jardinage faire des courses je dois... balayer débarrasser la table laver la voiture mettre le couvert passer l'aspirateur préparer les repas ranger ma chambre ranger la vaisselle sortir la poubelle tondre le gazon	I have to... do the ironing do the cooking do the washing do the washing-up I have to... go babysitting do the gardening go shopping I have to... sweep up clear the table wash the car lay the table do the hoovering get the meals ready tidy up my room put away the dishes put the bins out mow the lawn

La chambre	The bedroom
les meubles un placard un tiroir une armoire une coiffeuse une commode une étagère un lit un oreiller une couverture les rideaux un réveil une glace	furniture a cupboard a drawer a wardrobe a dressing table a chest of drawers a shelf a bed a pillow a blanket curtains an alarm clock a mirror

Le salon	The living room
un lecteur de disques compacts un magnétoscope une chaîne hi-fi une télé un canapé un coussin un fauteuil un tableau un tapis une lampe une pendule	a CD player a video recorder a stereo system a TV set a sofa a cushion an armchair a picture a rug a lamp a clock

Chapter 2 Chez moi

La cuisine	The kitchen
un congélateur un évier un four à micro-ondes un frigo un lave-vaisselle un sèche-linge une cuisinière à gaz une cuisinière électrique une machine à laver	a freezer a kitchen sink a microwave a fridge a dishwasher a dryer a gas cooker an electric cooker a washing machine

La salle à manger	The dining room
un buffet une chaise une table	a sideboard a chair a table

La salle de bains	The bathroom
un lavabo un robinet une baignoire une douche une toilette du dentifrice du savon une brosse à dents une brosse à cheveux une serviette	a washbasin a tap a bath a shower a toilet toothpaste soap a toothbrush a hairbrush a towel

Dans la chambre	In the bedroom
je dors j'écoute la radio j'écris des lettres je m'habille je lis je range mes affaires je me repose	I sleep I listen to the radio I write letters I get dressed I read I tidy up my things I have a rest

Dans le salon	In the living room
je bavarde ... avec mes frères ... avec mes sœurs j'écoute de la musique je joue aux cartes je regarde ... la télé ... des vidéos je me repose	I chat ... with my brothers ... with my sisters I listen to music I play cards I watch ... TV ... videos I have a rest

Chapter 2 Chez moi

Dans la cuisine	In the kitchen
j'aide ... ma mère ... mon père je fais ... la cuisine ... la lessive ... le repassage ... la vaisselle je prépare les repas je range la vaisselle	I help ... my mother ... my father I do ... the cooking ... the washing ... the ironing ... the washing-up I get the meals ready I put away the dishes

Dans la salle à manger	In the dining room
je débarrasse la table je mange je mets le couvert je prends le dîner	I clear the table I eat I lay the table I have my evening meal

Dans la salle de bains	In the bathroom
je me baigne je me brosse les dents je me brosse les cheveux je me douche je me lave je prends un bain	I have a bath I brush my teeth I brush my hair I have a shower I get washed I have a bath

Dans le jardin	In the garden
je me bronze je fais du jardinage je joue au foot je me repose je travaille	I sunbathe I do the gardening I play football I have rest I work

Les bâtiments	Buildings
un immeuble un appartement le rez-de-chaussée le premier étage le deuxième étage le troisième étage un balcon	a block of flats a flat the ground floor the first floor the second floor the third floor the balcony
une maison un garage un jardin un toit un arbre une cheminée une fenêtre une porte d'entrée des fleurs	a house a garage a garden a roof a tree a chimney a window a front door flowers

Chapter 3 Mes passe-temps

Que fais-tu pendant ton temps libre?	What do you do in your free time?
je fais ... du cheval ... du cyclisme ... du patinage ... du vélo ... de la danse ... de la gymnastique ... de la lecture ... de la natation ... de la photographie	I ... go horse-riding ... go cycling ... go skating ... go out on my bike ... go dancing ... do gymnastics ... read ... go swimming ... do some photography

je joue ... avec mon ordinateur ... au basket ... au cricket ... au foot ... au hockey ... au rugby ... au tennis ... aux cartes ... du clavier ... du piano ... de la guitare	I play ... on my computer ... basketball ... au cricket ... football ... hockey ... rugby ... tennis ... cards ... keyboard ... the piano ... the guitar

je collectionne des timbres j'écoute de la musique je regarde la télé je vais à la pêche	I collect stamps I listen to music I watch TV I go fishing

Chapter 3 Mes passe-temps

Qu'est-ce que tu as fait hier?	**What did you do yesterday?**
j'ai écouté mes cassettes	I listened to my cassettes
j'ai fait de l'équitation	I went horse-riding
j'ai fait de la natation	I went swimming
j'ai fait du vélo	I went out on my bike
j'ai joué au foot	I played football
j'ai joué du piano	I played the piano
j'ai lu un livre	I read a book
j'ai regardé la télé	I watched TV
j'ai vu un film	I saw a film
je suis allé (*m*) je suis allée (*f*)	I went
... à une boum	... to a party
... au cinéma	... to the cinema
je suis sorti (*m*) je suis sortie (*f*)	I went out
... avec mes amis	... with my friends
je suis resté (*m*) je suis restée (*f*)	I stayed
... chez moi	... at home

Qu'est-ce que tu feras demain?	**What are you going to do tomorrow?**
j'écouterai mes cassettes	I'll listen to my cassettes
je ferai de l'équitation	I'll go horse-riding
je ferai de la natation	I'll go swimming
je ferai du vélo	I'll go out on my bike
j'irai	I go
... à une boum	... to a party
... au cinéma	... to the cinema
je jouerai au foot	I'll play football
je jouerai du piano	I'll play the piano
je lirai un livre	I'll read a book
je regarderai la télé	I'll watch TV
je resterai	I'll stay
... chez moi	... at home
je sortirai	I go out
... avec mes amis	... with my friends
je verrai un film	I'll see a film

Chapter 3 Mes passe-temps – films/TV

Les films	Films
un dessin animé	a cartoon
un western	a western
un film	
... comique	a comedy
... d'amour	a love film
... d'aventure	an adventure film
... d'épouvante	a horror film
... de guerre	a war film
... d'horreur	a horror film
... policier	a thriller

Les émissions	TV programmes
un documentaire	a documentary
un feuilleton	a soap
un policier	a thriller
une émission sportive	a sports programme
une série dramatique	a series
le journal	the news
la météo	the weather forecast
les informations	the news
les jeux	quiz shows

j'adore … il / elle préfère … mes parents préfèrent …	nager
j'aime … mon frère aime …	jouer au tennis
je déteste … je n'aime pas … mon ami n'aime pas …	lire
C'est chouette	C'est moche

C'était super
- un très bon film
- amusant
- drôle / marrant

Ça m'a fait rire
Je l'ai trouvé chouette
J'ai adoré le film
Je l'ai beaucoup aimé
L' acteur / L' actrice joue bien

C'était un mauvais film

- ennuyeux
- trop violent
- sans imagination

Ça m'a agacé(e) / énervé(e)
Je l'ai trouvé bête
J'ai détesté le film
Je ne l'ai pas aimé
L' acteur / L' actrice ne joue pas bien

depuis	since
souvent	often
une fois	once
à partir de	from (in time)
jusqu'à	until
toujours	always
l'après-midi	afternoon
l'entrée	admission / entry fee
cher	expensive
interdit	forbidden
réduit	reduced
sauf	except
sportif	sporty (person)

le bal	ball / dance	la brochure	brochure
le balcon	balcony	la personne	person
le jour férié	public holiday	la place	seat
le programme	programme	la réduction	reduction
le spectacle	show	la salle	auditorium
le ticket	ticket	la séance	performance

Chapter 3 Mes passe-temps – inviting somebody out

tu veux aller...	would you like to go...
si on allait...	let's go/what about going...
... au café?	... to the café?
... au centre sportif?	... to the sports centre?
... au centre commercial?	... to the shopping centre?
... au cinéma?	... to the cinema?
... au marché?	... to the market?
... au musée?	... to the museum?
... au parc?	... to the park?
... au stade?	... to the stadium?
... au théâtre?	... to the theatre?
... à la boum?	... to the party?
... à la discothèque?	... to the disco?
... à la patinoire?	... to the ice rink?
... à la piscine?	... to the swimming pool?

danser	to dance
gagner	to win / earn
lire	to read
sortir	to go out
acheter	to buy
commencer	to begin / start
coûter	to cost
fermer	to close
ouvrir	to open
réserver	to reserve
trouver	to find

le basket	basketball
le club des jeunes	youth club
le compact disc (CD)	CD
le disque compact (CD)	CD
le disco	disco
le hockey	hockey
le jeu	game
le jeu vidéo	video game
le loisir	leisure
le match	match (football)
le membre	member (of a team)
le passe-temps	hobby
le roman	novel / book
le stade	stadium
le terrain (de foot)	(football) pitch

la cassette	cassette
la distraction	entertainment
l'équipe	team
l'orchestre	orchestra
l'ordinateur	computer
la pêche	fishing
la radio	radio
la surprise-partie	party

Chapter 4 En vacances

À l'hôtel	In the hotel
je voudrais une chambre ... ... avec balcon ... avec douche ... avec un grand lit ... avec deux lits ... avec salle de bains ... avec vue sur la mer ... au premier étage ... pour une personne ... pour deux personnes je voudrais une chambre de famille je voudrais ... la clé ... la note ... pension complète	I'd like a room... ... with a balcony ... with a shower ... with a double bed ... with two / twin beds ... with a bathroom ... with a view of the sea ... on the first floor ... for one person (a single room) ... for two people (a double room) I'd like a family room I'd like ... the key ... the bill ... full board (i.e. all meals included)

je ne suis pas content(e) il y a beaucoup de bruit il n'y a pas ... d'eau chaude ... de serviette le chauffage ne marche pas la douche ne marche pas	I'm not satisfied there is a lot of noise there isn't any ... hot water ... towel the heating doesn't work the shower doesn't work

est-ce qu'il y a ... un ascenseur? ... un parking? ... un restaurant à l'hôtel? ... un sèche-cheveux? ... un téléphone dans la chambre? ... un terrain de jeux?	is there ... a lift? ... a car park? ... a restaurant at the hotel? ... a hair-dryer? ... a telephone in the room? ... a playground?

Au camping	At the campsite
je voudrais un emplacement ... à l'ombre ... pour deux adultes et trois enfants ... pour une caravane ... pour une tente est-ce qu'il y a ... un parking? ... un restaurant? ... une alimentation? ... une boulangerie? ... une épicerie? est-ce qu'on peut ... allumer un feu? ... faire un barbecue? oui non, c'est interdit	I'd like a plot ... in the shade ... for two adults and three children ... for a caravan ... for a tent is there ... a car park? ... a restaurant? ... a food shop? ... a baker's? ... a food shop? are you allowed to ... light a fire? ... have a barbecue? yes no, it's not allowed

Chapter 4 En vacances

À l'auberge de jeunesse	At the youth hostel
vous avez de la place ... pour une fille et un garçon? c'est pour deux nuits c'est pour une semaine voici ma carte (de membre) où sont ... les dortoirs des filles? ... les dortoirs des garçons? ... les lavabos? ... les toilettes? à quelle heure ferme l'auberge? il y a une tâche à faire? je peux louer un sac de couchage?	do you have room ... for a girl and a boy? it's for two nights it's for a week here's my (membership) card where are ... the girls' dormitories? ... the boys' dormitories? ... the washbasins? ... the toilets? what time does the hostel close? is there a task / chore to do? can I hire / borrow a sleeping bag?

Chapter 5 Mes vacances

j'ai fait	
... du camping	I went camping
... du shopping	I went shopping
... du vélo	I went out on my bike
... la grasse matinée	I slept in
... la cuisine	I did the cooking
... des barbecues	I had barbecues
j'ai joué au tennis	I played tennis
j'ai joué au volleyball	I played volleyball
j'ai lu	I read
j'ai mangé au restaurant	I ate in a restaurant
j'ai visité des monuments historiques	I visited places of historical interest
j'ai vu des feux d'artifice	I saw firework displays
je suis allé (*m*) je suis allée (*f*)	I went
... au cirque	... to the circus
... au marché	... to the market
... à la discothèque	... to the disco
... à la pêche	... fishing
... à la plage	... to the beach
je suis sorti (*m*) je suis sortie (*f*)	I went out
... avec mes amis	... with my friends
je me suis bronzé (*m*) je me suis bronzée (*f*)	I sunbathed
je me suis promené (*m*) je me suis promenée (*f*)	I went out walking
je me suis reposé (*m*) je me suis reposée (*f*)	I had a rest

je ferai	
... du camping	I'll go camping
... du shopping	I'll go shopping
... du vélo	I'll go out on my bike
... la grasse matinée	I'll sleep in
... la cuisine	I'll do the cooking
... des barbecues	I'll have barbecues
je jouerai au tennis	I'll play tennis
je jouerai au volleyball	I'll play volleyball
je lirai	I'll read
je mangerai au restaurant	I'll eat in a restaurant
je visiterai des monuments historiques	I'll visit places of historical interest
je verrai des feux d'artifice	I'll see firework displays
j'irai	I'll go
... au cirque	... to the circus
... au marché	... to the market
... à la discothèque	... to the disco
... à la pêche	... fishing
... à la plage	... to the beach
je sortirai	I'll go out
... avec mes amis	... with my friends
je me bronzerai	I'll sunbathe
je me promènerai	I'll go out walking
je me reposerai	I'll have a rest

Chapter 5 Mes vacances

La météo	The weather forecast
il fait beau il fait chaud il fait froid il fait mauvais il fait soleil il fait du brouillard il fait du vent il fait un temps couvert	the weather's fine the weather's hot the weather's cold the weather's bad it's sunny it's foggy it's windy it's overcast
il gèle il neige il pleut	it's freezing it's snowing it's raining
il y a de l'orage	it's thundery

Les pays	Countries
le Canada le Danemark le Pays de Galles le Portugal	Canada Denmark Wales Portugal
l'Angleterre l'Autriche la Belgique l'Écosse l'Espagne la Finlande la France la Grèce l'Irlande l'Italie la Pologne la Suède la Suisse	England Austria Belgium Scotland Spain Finland France Greece Irland Italy Poland Sweden Switzerland
les États-Unis les Pays-Bas	the USA the Netherlands (Holland)

Chapter 5 Mes vacances

Les nationalités		Nationalities
masculin	*féminin*	
américain	américaine	American
anglais	anglaise	English
écossais	écossaise	Scottish
finlandais	finlandaise	Finnish
français	française	French
hollandais	hollandaise	Dutch
irlandais	irlandaise	Irish
polonais	polonaise	Polish
portugais	portugaise	Portuguese
danois	danoise	Danish
gallois	galloise	Welsh
suédois	suédoise	Swedish
autrichien	autrichienne	Austrian
canadien	canadienne	Canadian
italien	italienne	Italian
belge	belge	Belgian
suisse	suisse	Swiss
espagnol	espagnole	Spanish
grec	grecque	Greek

quel temps fait-il?	what's the weather like?
geler	to freeze
neiger	to snow
pleuvoir	to rain
le nuage	cloud
le temps	weather
la glace	ice
la météo	weather forecast
je suis allé(e) en France (en for feminine country)	
je suis allé(e) au Portugal (au for masculine country)	
je suis allé(e) aux Etats-Unis (aux for plural country)	

Chapter 6 En ville – transport/places

je vais...	I go / I'm going...
je voyage...	I travel / I'm travelling...
... à bicyclette	... by bike
... à cheval	... on horseback
... à pied	... on foot
... en auto	... by car
... en avion	... by plane
... en bateau	... by boat
... en bus	... by bus
... en camion	... by lorry
... en car	... by coach
... en hovercraft / en aéroglisseur	... by hovercraft
... en moto	... by motorbike
... en scooter	... by moped
... en train	... by train
... en vélo	... by bike
... en voiture	... by car
... par le ferry	... by ferry

pour aller...	can you tell me the way...
... au centre sportif	... to the sports centre
... au château	... to the castle
... au cinéma	... to the cinema
... au jardin public	... to the park
... au musée	... to the museum
... au supermarché	... to the supermarket
... au syndicat d'initiative	... to the tourist office
... au théâtre	... to the theatre
... à la banque	... to the bank
... à la bibiothèque	... to the library
... à la cathédrale	... to the cathedral
... à la gare	... to the station
... à la gare routière	... to the bus station
... à la mairie	... to the town hall
... à la piscine	... to the swimming pool
... à l'église	... to the church
... à l'hôtel de ville	... to the town hall
... à l'office de tourisme	... to the tourist office
s'il vous plaît?	please?

Chapter 6 En ville – transport/places

À la gare	At the railway station
le buffet le bureau ... d'objets trouvés ... de poste ... de renseignements	the buffet / café the lost property office the post office the travel centre / information
la consigne la consigne automatique la sortie	the left luggage office the left luggage lockers the exit
les guichets pour billet	the ticket office
eau potable fumeur non fumeur réservation toilettes dames toilettes hommes	drinking water smoking non-smoking reservation women's toilets men's toilets

je prends ... le bus ... le car ... le train ... le bateau ... le ferry je prends ... la voiture	
tournez à droite tournez à gauche allez tout droit traversez … je voudrais un aller simple à Paris en première classe je voudrais un aller-retour à Paris en deuxième classe	turn right turn left go straight ahead cross …
N'oubliez pas de composter votre billet Departs – grandes lignes Departs banlieues c'est direct? Quais Acces aux quais Il est interdit de traverser la voie Correspondances En provenance de … A destination de … Indicateurs / horaires	don't forget to stamp your ticket main line / intercity departures local departures is it direct? platforms to the trains it is forbidden to cross the track connections trains coming from … trains going to … timetables

Chapter 7 On fait des achats – shopping, shops and food

avez-vous... ? je voudrais... donnez-moi s'il vous plaît...	do you have... ? I'd like... please give me...

A la boucherie	**At the butcher's**
... de l'agneau ... du bœuf ... du porc ... du poulet	... some lamb ... some beef ... some pork ... some chicken

A la boulangerie	**At the baker's**
... du pain ... un croissant ... un gâteau ... une baguette ... une pâtisserie	... some bread ... a croissant ... a cake ... a baguette / French stick ... a cream cake

A l'épicerie	**At the general grocer**
... de l'eau minérale ... de la limonade ... des biscuits ... des bonbons ... des chips ... des petits gâteaux ... des œufs ... des yaourts	... some mineral water ... some lemonade ... some biscuits ... some sweets ... some crisps ... some biscuits ... some eggs ... some yoghurts

A la poissonnerie	**At the fish shop**
... du poisson ... des fruits de mer	... some fish ... some seafood (shrimps, mussels, etc)

Chez le marchand de fruits	**At the fruit shop**
... un ananas ... un melon ... un pamplemousse ... des abricots ... des bananes ... des cerises ... des fraises ... des framboises ... des oranges ... des pêches ... des pommes ... du raisin	... a pineapple ... a melon ... a grapefruit ... some apricots ... some bananas ... some cherries ... some strawberries ... some raspberries ... some oranges ... some peaches ... some apples ... some grapes

Chapter 7 On fait des achats – shopping, shops and food

Chez le marchand de légumes	At the vegetable shop
... un chou ... un chou-fleur ... une salade ... des carottes ... des champignons ... des haricots verts ... des oignons ... des petits pois ... des poivrons ... des pommes de terre ... des tomates	... a cabbage ... a cauliflower ... a lettuce ... some carrots ... some mushrooms ... some green beans ... some onions ... some peas ... some peppers ... some potatoes ... some tomatoes

Chapter 7 On fait des achats – quantities

je voudrais... ... un demi kilo de raisin ... un kilo de tomates ... un morceau de fromage ... un paquet de café ... un pot de yaourt	I'd like ... half a kilo of grapes ... a kilo of tomatoes ... a piece of cheese ... a packet of coffee ... a pot of yoghurt

je voudrais... ... une boîte de limonade ... une boîte de carottes ... une livre de pêches ... une bouteille de jus d'orange ... une portion de frites ... une tranche de jambon ... une douzaine d'œufs	I'd like ... a can of lemonade ... a tin of carrots ... a pound of peaches ... a bottle of orange juice ... a portion of chips ... a slice of ham ... a dozen eggs

Les vêtements	**Clothes**
un chemisier un collant un imperméable un jean un jogging un maillot de bain un manteau un pantalon un pull un short un soutien-gorge un sweat un T-shirt	a blouse a pair of tights a raincoat a pair of jeans a jogging outfit swimming trunks / a swimming costume a coat a pair of trousers a pullover a pair of shorts a bra a sweatshirt a tee shirt

une chemise une cravate une jupe une robe une veste	a shirt a tie a skirt a dress a formal jacket

des baskets des chaussettes des chaussures	trainers socks shoes

Chapter 7 On fait des achats – at the post office/bank

A la poste	At the post office
un timbre pour l'Angleterre un timbre à 0,50 euros il y a une cabine téléphonique? où sont les téléphones? où est la boîte aux lettres? je voudrais une télécarte je voudrais téléphoner en P.C.V. je voudrais envoyer ... une lettre aux Pays de Galles ... une lettre par avion ... une carte postale en Angleterre ... un paquet en Écosse quand est-ce que la lettre arrivera?	a stamp for England a stamp for 50 cents / 0.50 euros is there a phone box? where are the telephones? where is the letter box? I'd like a phone card I'd like to make a reverse charge call I'd like to send ... a letter to Wales ... an airmail letter ... a postcard to England ... a parcel to Scotland when will the letter arrive?

A la banque	At the bank
je voudrais changer un chèque je voudrais changer 20 livres sterling dans quelle devise? j'aimerais des pièces d'un euro j'aimerais des billets de cent euro avez-vous une pièce d'identité? oui, voici mon passeport	I'd like to change a cheque I'd like to change 20 pounds into which currency? I'd like one euro coins I'd like hundred euro notes do you have a document to confirm your identity? yes, here's my passport

Chapter 8 Au café / Au restaurant

Les casse-croûtes	Snacks
du gâteau	some cake
un croque-monsieur	a cheese and ham toastie
un hot-dog	a hot dog
un sandwich	
... au fromage	a cheese sandwich
... au jambon	a ham sandwich
... au pâté	a paté sandwich
... au poulet	a chicken sandwich
... au saucisson	a salami sandwich
une crêpe	a pancake
une pizza	a pizza
une quiche	a quiche
des frites	chips

Les boissons	Drinks
du champagne	some champagne
du lait	some milk
du vin	some wine
un café crème	coffee with cream
un café au lait	a white coffee
un chocolat chaud	a hot chocolate
un chocolat froid	a cold chocolate
un cidre	a cider
un coca	a coke
un jus de fruit	a fruit juice
un thé au citron	tea with lemon
un thé au lait	tea with milk
un vin blanc	a white wine
un vin rouge	a red wine
une bière	a beer
une eau minérale	a mineral water
une limonade	a lemonade
une orange pressée	fresh orange juice

A table	At the table
je voudrais	I'd like
... le poivre	... the pepper
... le sel	... the salt
... le sucre	... the sugar
... le vinaigre	... the vinegar
... la moutarde	... the mustard
... la mayonnaise	... the mayonnaise
s'il vous plaît	please

Chapter 8 Au café / Au restaurant

Comme entrée	As a starter
je prends... je voudrais... ... le melon ... le pâté ... le potage ... le saucisson ... la soupe ... les crudités	I'll take... I'd like... ... melon ... paté ... soup ... salami sausage ... soup ... plate of salad / raw vegetables

Comme plat principal	As a main course
je prends... je voudrais... ... l'agneau ... le bifteck ... le canard ... le jambon ... le lapin ... le mouton ... le poisson ... le poulet ... le rôti de porc ... le veau ... la dinde ... la truite ... une côtelette de porc ... les crevettes ... les moules	I'll take... I'd like... ... lamb ... a beef steak ... duck ... ham ... rabbit ... mutton ... fish ... chicken ... roast pork ... veal ... turkey ... trout ... a pork chop ... prawns ... mussels

Comme dessert	As a dessert
je prends... je voudrais... ... le fromage ... le gâteau ... le yaourt ... une crêpe ... la glace à la fraise ... la glace à la framboise ... la glace à la vanille ... la tarte aux cerises ... la tarte aux pommes	I'll take... I'd like... ... cheese ... cake ... yoghurt ... a pancake ... a strawberry ice cream ... a raspberry ice cream ... a vanilla ice cream ... cherry tart ... apple tart

Chapter 8 Au café / Au restaurant

A table	At the table
un couteau un verre une assiette une cuillère une fourchette une tasse l'addition la carte	a knife a glass a plate a spoon a fork a cup the bill the menu

Des problèmes	Problems
l'assiette est sale le potage est froid je n'ai pas de verre j'attends depuis 30 minutes	the plate is dirty the soup is cold I don't have a glass I've been waiting for 30 minutes

Chapter 9 Au collège

Au collège il y a	At school there is
un centre sportif un terrain de foot	a sports centre a football pitch
une bibliothèque une cantine une cour une piscine une salle de gym une salle d'informatique une salle des professeurs	a library a canteen a playground a swimming pool a gym a computer suite / room a staffroom
des ateliers des courts de tennis des laboratoires de langue des laboratoires de sciences des salles de classe des salles préfabriquées des vestiaires	workshops tennis courts language laboratories science laboratories classrooms prefabs / portakabins / terrapins changing rooms

Les matières scolaires	School subjects
j'aime... j'adore... je préfère... je n'aime pas... je déteste...	I like... I love... I prefer... I don't like... I hate...
... l'allemand ... l'anglais ... le commerce ... le dessin ... l'espagnol ... le français ... l'italien ... le russe ... le sport	... German ... English ... economics ... art ... Spanish ... French ... Italian ... Russian ... sport
... la biologie ... la chimie ... l'éducation physique ... l'éducation religieuse ... la géographie ... la gymnastique ... l'histoire ... l'informatique ... la musique ... la physique ... la technologie	... biology ... chemistry ... P.E. (physical education) ... R.E. (religious education) ... geography ... gym ... history ... I.C.T ... music ... physics ... technology
... les langues vivantes ... les mathématiques ... les SDVT*	... modern languages ... maths ... science

**SDVT = Sciences de la Vie et de la Terre*

Chapter 10 Au travail – jobs

Les métiers		Jobs
je voudrais être...		I'd like to be...
ma mère est...		my mother is...
ma sœur est...		my sister is...
mon père est...		my father is...
mon frère est...		my brother is...
... agent de police		... a police officer
... dactylo		... a shorthand typist
... dentiste		... a dentist
... élève		... a pupil
... garagiste		... a garage owner / mechanic
... médecin		... a doctor
... professeur		... a (secondary school) teacher
... secrétaire		... a secretary
masculin	*féminin*	
avocat	avocate	... a lawyer
étudiant	étudiante	... a student
patron	patronne	... a boss / manager
boulanger	boulangère	... a baker
boucher	bouchère	... a butcher
caissier	caissière	... a check-out attendant
cuisinier	cuisinière	... a cook / chef
épicier	épicière	... a grocer / shopkeeper
fermier	fermière	... a farmer
infirmier	infirmière	... a nurse
ouvrier	ouvrière	... a (factory) worker
pompier	pompière	... a fire officer
chauffeur de taxi	chauffeuse de taxi	... a taxi driver
coiffeur	coiffeuse	... a hairdresser / barber
serveur	serveuse	... a waiter / waitress
vendeur	vendeuse	... a shop assistant
facteur	factrice	... a postman / postlady
instituteur	institutrice	... a (primary school) teacher
électricien	électricienne	... an electrician
informaticien	informaticienne	... a computer engineer
mécanicien	mécanicienne	... a mechanic
steward	hôtesse de l'air	... an air steward / air hostess
garçon de café		... a waiter
je suis au chômage		I'm unemployed
il / elle est au chômage		he / she is unemployed

The international world

Greenpeace	
veut protéger la nature veut protéger l'environnement	wants to protect nature wants to protect the environment

La croix rouge	The Red Cross
apporte de l'aide dans le monde apporte de l'aide aux réfugiés veut secourir les blessés de guerre	provides help throughout the world provides help to refugees wants to help those wounded in war

Médecins Sans Frontières (MSF)	
apporte de l'assistance médicale ... où il y a des catastrophes naturelles ... où il y a des guerres	provides medical assistance ... where there are natural catastrophes ... where there are wars

L'Unesco	Unesco
essaie de développer ... la culture ... l'éducation ... la science essaie de maintenir la paix... essaie d'encourager la collaboration... ... entre les pays	tries to develop / promote ... culture ... education ... science tries to keep the peace... tries to encourage co-operation... ... between countries

SPA	
agit contre la cruauté envers les animaux agit pour la protection des animaux	acts against cruelty to animals acts for the protection of animals

Amnesty International	
apporte aide... ... aux prisonniers ... ... aux victimes ... ... qui souffrent à cause de leurs croyances	provides help... ... to prisoners ... ... to victims ... ... who suffer because of their beliefs

Les Restos du Cœur	
donne à manger aux personnes SDF (sans domicile fixe)	provides food for homeless people

The international world

Problèmes	Problems
le chômage le racisme le S.I.D.A la faim la guerre la pauvreté la violence ... dans les cités ... dans les écoles ... dans les villes l'environnement: les automobiles l'effet de serre l'énergie nucléaire le recyclage la drogue (se droguer) le tabagisme (fumer) l'abus d'alcool (boire)	unemployment racism AIDS hunger / famine war poverty violence ... in big housing estates ... in schools ... in towns the environment: cars the greenhouse effect nuclear energy recycling drugs (to take drugs) smoking (to smoke) alcohol abuse (to drink)

Causes	Causes
le climat l'ennui le manque d'espoir le manque d'argent le surpeuplement l'avidité nos besoins nos habitudes	climate boredom lack of hope lack of money overpopulation greed our needs our habits

Solutions	Solutions
il faut... ... changer nos habitudes ... être moins egoïste ... faire des efforts ... s'informer ... lutter (contre) ... secourir les gens il faut... ... créer des pistes cyclables ... marcher ... multiplier les transports en commun je veux protéger ma planète	we'll have to... ... change our habits ... be less selfish ... make an effort ... be better informed ... fight / struggle (against) ... help people we'll have to... ... create cycle tracks ... walk ... increase public transport I want to protect my planet

The international world

Les opinions	Opinions
je suis contre... je suis pour... je pense que... je trouve que... il me semble que...	I'm against... I'm for... I think that... I think that... it seems to me that...
je me fais des soucis... je m'intéresse à...	I'm worried about... I'm interested in...
je suis optimiste je suis pessimiste ça me préoccupe ça me concerne	I'm optimistic I'm pessimistic I'm worried about it I'm concerned about it

apporter de l'aide	to bring help / assistance
secourir	to help
maintenir	to maintain
guérir	to cure
menacer	to threaten
soigner les malades	to care for the sick
tuer	to kill
éliminer	to eliminate
protéger	to protect
le tiers monde	third world
le pays	country
les pays en voie de développement	developing countries
les droits	rights
la souffrance	suffering
la guerre	war
la religion	religion
la paix	peace
la catastrophe	catastrophe
la victime	victim
la faim	hunger
la pénurie (d'eau)	shortage (of water)
la cruauté	cruelty
les croyances	beliefs
les SDF (sans domicile fixe)	homeless

General

Les numéros	Numbers
zéro	0
un, deux, trois, quatre, cinq	1, 2, 3, 4, 5
six, sept, huit, neuf, dix	6, 7, 8, 9, 10
onze, douze, treize	11, 12, 13
quatorze, quinze, seize	14, 15, 16
dix-sept, dix-huit, dix-neuf	17, 18, 19
vingt	20
vingt et un, vingt-deux, vingt-trois, ...	21, 22, 23, ...
trente	30
trente et un, trente-deux, trente-trois, ...	31, 32, 33, ...
quarante	40
cinquante	50
soixante	60
soixante-dix	70
soixante et onze, soixante-douze, ...	71, 72, ...
quatre-vingts	80
quatre-vingt-un, quatre-vingt-deux, ...	81, 82, ...
quatre-vingt-dix	90
quatre-vingt-onze, quatre-vingt-douze, ...	91, 92, ...
cent	100
deux cents, trois cents, cinq cents	200, 300, 500
cinq cent quarante	540
mille	1000
deux mille	2000

Les jours de la semaine	Days of the week
lundi	Monday
mardi	Tuesday
mercredi	Wednesday
jeudi	Thursday
vendredi	Friday
samedi	Saturday
dimanche	Sunday

une semaine	a week
un mois	a month
une nuit	a night
un jour	a day

Les mois de l'année	Months of the year
janvier	January
février	February
mars	March
avril	April
mai	May
juin	June
juillet	July
août	August
septembre	September
octobre	October
novembre	November
décembre	December

Grammar

The Perfect Tense

Verbs in the perfect tense need:
1 the auxiliary verb avoir *or* être
2 the past participle

***Pattern with* avoir**			**_Examples_**	
j'ai		-er *verbs:* manger mangé	j'ai mangé	I ate
tu as			ils ont mangé	they ate
il/elle/on a	+	-ir *verbs:* finir fini	nous avons fini	we finished
nous avons			vous avez fini?	have you finished?
vous avez		-re *verbs:* vendre vendu	tu as vendu?	did you sell?
ils/elles ont			elle a vendu	she sold

avoir	j'ai eu	to have	I had	ouvrir	j'ai ouvert	to open	I opened
boire	j'ai bu	to drink	I drank	pouvoir	j'ai pu	to be able to	I was able to
courir	j'ai couru	to run	I ran	prendre	j'ai pris	to take	I took
devoir	j'ai dû	to have to	I had to	recevoir	j'ai reçu	to get	I got
dire	j'ai dit	to say	I said	rire	j'ai ri	to laugh	I laughed
écrire	j'ai écrit	to write	I wrote	savoir	j'ai su	to know	I knew
faire	j'ai fait	to do	I did	voir	j'ai vu	to see	I saw
lire	j'ai lu	to read	I read				
mettre	j'ai mis	to put	I put				

***Pattern with* être**			**_Examples_**	
		(*masc. sing.*)	je suis allé	I went (*m*)
je suis		+ allé	je suis allée	I went (*f*)
tu es		(*fem. sing.*) + *e*	tu es allé?	you went (*m*)
il/elle/on est	+	+ allée	elle est allée	she went (*f*)
nous sommes		(*masc. plural*) + *s*	nous sommes allées	we went (*f*)
vous êtes		+ allés	vous êtes allés?	you went (*m*)
ils/elles sont		(*fem. plural*) + *es*	ils sont allés	they went (*m*)
		+ allées	elles sont allées	they went (*f*)

monter	to go up	il est monté, elle est montée	he/she went up
rester	to stay	il est resté, elle est restée	he/she stayed
venir	to come	il est venu, elle est venue	he/she came
aller	to go	il est allé, elle est allée	he/she went
naître	to be born	il est né, elle est née	he/she was born
descendre	to go down	il est descendu, elle est descendue	he/she went down
entrer	to go in	il est entré, elle est entrée	he/she went in
retourner	to go back	il est retourné, elle est retournée	he/she went back
sortir	to go out	il est sorti, elle est sortie	he/she went out
tomber	to fall	il est tombé, elle est tombée	he/she fell
arriver	to arrive	il est arrivé, elle est arrivée	he/she arrived
mourir	to die	il est mort, elle est mort	he/she died
partir	to leave	il est parti, elle est partie	he/she left

Grammar

Time markers	
ce matin hier hier matin hier soir le week-end dernier la semaine dernière l'année dernière	this morning yesterday yesterday morning yesterday evening last weekend last week last year

The Present Tense

-er verbs: pattern	*Example*	
-e -es -e -ons -ez -ent	je donne tu donnes il/elle/on donne nous donnons vous donnez ils/elles donnent	I give you give he/she/we give we give you give they give

-ir verbs: pattern	*Example*	
-is -is -it -issons -issez -issent	je finis tu finis il/elle/on finit nous finissons vous finissez ils/elles finissent	I finish you finish he/she/we finish we finish you finish they finish

-re verbs: pattern	*Example*	
-s -s - -ons -ez -ent	je vends tu vends il/elle/on vend nous vendons vous vendez ils/elles vendent	I sell you sell he/she/we sell we sell you sell they sell

reflexive verbs			
je me lave tu te laves il se lave elle se lave nous nous lavons vous vous lavez ils/elles se lavent	I wash myself you wash yourself he washes himself she washes herself we wash ourselves you wash yourselves they wash themselves	je me couche tu te couches il se couche elle se couche nous nous couchons vous vous couchez ils/elles se couchent	I go to bed you go to bed he goes to bed she goes to bed we go to bed you go to bed they go to bed

Grammar

Irregular verbs			
avoir	to have	être	to be
j'ai	I have	je suis	I am
tu as	you have	tu es	you are
il/elle/on a	he/she/we have	il/elle/on est	he/she is, we are
nous avons	we have	nous sommes	we are
vous avez	you have	vous êtes	you are
ils/elles ont	they have	ils/elles sont	they are
aller	to go	faire	to do
je vais	I go	je fais	I do
tu vas	you go	tu fais	you do
il/elle/on va	he/she/we go	il/elle/on fait	he/she/we do
nous allons	we go	nous faisons	we do
vous allez	you go	vous faites	you do
ils/elles vont	they go	ils/elles font	they do
appeler	to call	dormir	to sleep
j'appelle	I call	je dors	I sleep
tu appelles	you call	tu dors	you sleep
il/elle/on appelle	he/she/we call	il/elle/on dort	he/she/we sleep
nous appelons	we call	nous dormons	we sleep
vous appellez	you call	vous dormez	you sleep
ils/elles appellent	they call	ils/elles dorment	they sleep
mettre	to put	prendre	to take
je mets	I put	je prends	I take
tu mets	you put	tu prends	you take
il/elle/on met	he/she/we put	il/elle/on prend	he/she/we take
nous mettons	we put	nous prenons	we take
vous mettez	you put	vous prenez	you take
ils/elles mettent	they put	ils/elles prennent	they take
venir	to come		
je viens	I come		
tu viens	you come		
il/elle/on vient	he/she/we come		
nous venons	we come		
vous venez	you come		
ils/elles viennent	they come		

Time markers	
aujourd'hui	today
normalement	normally
d'habitude	usually
maintenant	now
souvent	often
tous les jours	every day
tous les soirs	every evening

Grammar

The Future Tense

1 = *going to. Use* aller + *infinitive*

Pattern			*Examples*	
je vais			je vais manger	I'm going to eat
tu vas		*infinitive:*	tu vas boire	you're going to drink
il/elle/on va	+	*-er*	il va aller	he's going to go
nous allons		*-ir*	nous allons finir	we're going to finish
vous allez		*-re*	vous allez partir	you're going to leave
ils/elles vont			elles vont arriver	they're going to arrive

2 *Future Tense. Add the following endings to the infinitive stem*

		ai
		as
infinitive	+	a
		ons
		ez
		ont

Add the endings to the infinitive

donner	**to give**
je donnerai	I'll give
tu donneras	you'll give
il/elle/on donnera	he/she/we'll give
nous donnerons	we'll give
vous donnerez	you'll give
ils/elles donneront	they'll give

finir	**to finish**
je finirai	I'll finish
tu finiras	you'll finish
il/elle/on finira	he/she/we'll finish
nous finirons	we'll finish
vous finirez	you'll finish
ils/elles finiront	they'll finish

Add the endings to the infinitive -e

vendre	**to sell**
je vendrai	I'll sell
tu vendras	you'll sell
il/elle/on vendra	he/she/we'll sell
nous vendrons	we'll sell
vous vendrez	you'll sell
ils/elles vendront	they'll sell

Exceptions: same endings – it's the first part of the verb (the stem) that's irregular

acheter	to buy	j'achèterai	I'll buy
aller	to go	j'irai	I'll go
appeler	to call	j'appellerai	I'll call
avoir	to have	j'aurai	I'll have
courir	to run	je courrai	I'll run
devoir	to have to	je devrai	I'll have to
envoyer	to send	j'enverrai	I'll send
être	to be	je serai	I'll be
faire	to do	je ferai	I'll do
mourir	to die	je mourrai	I'll die
pouvoir	to be able to	je pourrai	I'll be able to
recevoir	to get	je recevrai	I'll get
savoir	to know	je saurai	I'll know
venir	to come	je viendrai	I'll come
voir	to see	je verrai	I'll see
vouloir	to want to	je voudrai	I'll want to

Time markers	
ce soir	this evening
demain	tomorrow
la semaine prochaine	next week
l'année prochaine	next year

Quelle heure est-il?

Time past the hour

Il est deux heures.

Il est deux heures cinq.

Il est deux heures dix.

Il est deux heures et quart.

Il est deux heures vingt.

Il est deux heures vingt-cinq.

Il est deux heures et demie.

Time to the hour

Il est trois heures moins vingt-cinq.

Il est trois heures moins vingt.

Il est trois heures moins le quart.

Il est trois heures moins dix.

Il est midi.

Il est minuit.

Il est midi et quart.

Il est midi et demi.

Digital time

Il est sept heures dix.

Il est sept heures quinze.

Il est sept heures trente.

Il est sept heures quarante-cinq.

Be careful with 7 p.m. = dix-neuf heures!

AM and PM

8 am = 8 heures du matin

8 pm = 8 heures du soir

At + time

At 3 pm = à 15 heures *or* à 3 heures de l'après midi.

At 5 am = à 5 heures *or* à 5 heures du matin.

Before you start

The four exam papers covered here – there's one for each skill – each have three parts: if you are aiming for the Foundation tier, do the Foundation (F) and Foundation / Higher (F/H) parts, but if you are aiming for the Higher tier, do the Foundation / Higher (F/H) and Higher (H) parts.

But remember that in the exam you will get a booklet for the exam tier for which you have been entered: Foundation or Higher. So make sure you do all the activities in the examination booklet – don't miss anything out!

Make sure you know all the possible instructions listed on pages 4–5.

The four skills

Listening

Your mock exam is on the CD available with this study guide.

The pauses are timed so that you keep the CD playing – don't stop it once you've started. You should also check with your teacher to see if the awarding body with which you are entered uses timed pauses (e.g. OCR) , or whether the teacher will stop the CD for pauses (e.g. AQA).

On your CD, the first part is the Foundation, then the Foundation / Higher and finally the Higher. So if you're doing the Higher tier, you'll have to go to the start of the Foundation / Higher part.

Speaking

Give yourself 15 minutes to prepare your two role play activities. If you are entering an AQA or OCR exam, prepare your Presentation. Record yourself if possible.

Reading

Allow yourself approximately 50 minutes to complete the two parts.

Writing

Check your work carefully. Allow yourself about an hour to complete the two parts.

Listening F

Exercice 1 Au café

Choisissez la bonne image.
Ecrivez la lettre dans la case.

A 

B 

C 

D 

E 

F 

G 

H 

I 

J 

Ecoutez l'exemple.

Exemple = [I]

1 = ☐

2 = ☐

3 = ☐ + ☐

4 = ☐ + ☐ [6]

Exercice 2 Les passe-temps

Ecoutez les préférences sportives de David, Mylène et André.
Cochez deux cases pour chaque personne.
Ecoutez l'exemple de David.

David	✓							✓
Mylène								
André								

[4]

Exercise 3

You are going to Paris to stay with Anne, a French friend.

Answer each question by ticking one box only.

Example:

At the station
The train leaves from platform ...?

A ☐

B ☐

C ☐

D ☑

1 At the station
How late is your train (in minutes)?

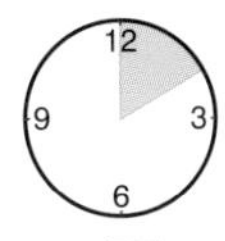

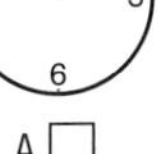

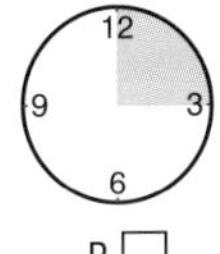

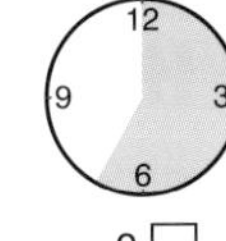

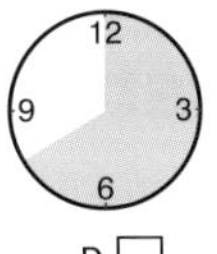

A ☐ B ☐ C ☐ D ☐

2 Meeting Anne
How does Anne suggest getting home?

A ☐ B ☐ C ☐ D ☐

3 At Anne's house
Anne asks if you would like to ...?

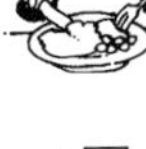

A ☐ B ☐ C ☐ D ☐

4 At Anne's house
What does Anne suggest doing tonight?

A ☐ 

C ☐ 

B ☐ 

D ☐ 

[4]

Exercice 4

Vous allez entendre la météo pour la France deux fois.

Choisissez la bonne lettre pour chaque région.

A 

B 

C 

D 

E 

F 

G 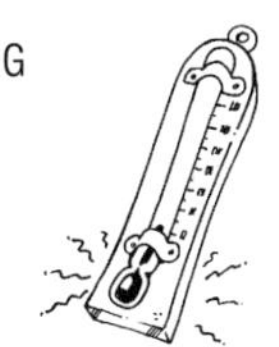

H 

Exemple: Normandie = H

1 Région parisienne = _

2 Massif Central = _

3 Bretagne = _

4 Alpes = _

5 Languedoc = _

6 Alsace = _

[6]

Listening F/H

Complete these exercises if you are doing the Foundation or the Higher tier.

Exercise 1

You are working in a hotel. A French person leaves a message on the answerphone to make a booking. Fill in the reservation details for your boss in *English*.

You will hear the message twice.

Name: Monsieur ....

Room details double ☐ single ☐ (tick one)
shower ☐ bathroom ☐ (tick one)

Proposed dates of stay:

from .... to ....

Special requirements:

....

[4]

Exercice 2 Un échange scolaire

Vous allez entendre deux fois le programme d'activités d'un échange scolaire.
Complétez les notes en français.

Echange scolaire - programme d'activités

lundi	*Plage* Rendez-vous à 9h 15 N'oubliez pas ______________
mardi	*Réception officielle* Où? ______________ Rendez-vous à ______ h ______
mercredi	*Journée en famille* Le soir, activité ______________
jeudi	*Aqualand* N'oubliez pas __________ Départ à 8h 30. Rendez-vous où? ______________
vendredi	*Carcassonne – ville médiévale* Activités i______________ ii ______________ N'oubliez pas ______________
samedi	*Départ des Anglais* Rendez-vous à 15h 30. Où? ______________

[10]

Exercice 3 Les vacances!

Vous allez entendre deux fois, deux jeunes, Marc et Nathalie.
Répondez aux questions en cochant la bonne case, A, B ou C.
D'abord, lisez les questions.

1 Nathalie est allée ...

A ☐ en Espagne.
B ☐ à une station balnéaire.
C ☐ à la campagne.

2 Nathalie et Catrine ont séjourné ...

A ☐ dans un camping.
B ☐ dans un petit appartement.
C ☐ dans une auberge de jeunesse.

3 Au début de leurs vacances, il a fait ...

A ☐ beau.
B ☐ froid.
C ☐ un temps orageux.

4 Nathalie dit que l'année dernière, les prix des locations étaient ...

A ☐ raisonnables.
B ☐ bon marché.
C ☐ chers.

5 Le matin, Nathalie et Catrine ...

A ☐ restaient au lit.
B ☐ allaient à la plage.
C ☐ se promenaient en ville.

6 Selon Nathalie, quel était le seul inconvénient des vacances?

A ☐ Elles étaient loin de la mer.
B ☐ Les restaurants fermaient de bonne heure.
C ☐ Elles logeaient dans un quartier bruyant.

[6]

Listening H

Complete these exercises only if you are doing the Higher tier.

Exercice 1 Le surf

Vous allez entendre deux fois une interview avec Jérémy.

Il habite et surfe à la Martinique.

Complétez les phrases suivantes en français.

Regardez l'exemple.

Jérémy a eu sa première petite planche *à l'âge de 2 ans.*

1 Il aime le surf parce qu'il aime ....

2 A la Martinique, il s'entraîne ....

3 Il pense que le surf des neiges était ....

4 Pour faire du surf, il faut .... et connaître les vagues.

5 A son avis, la mode surf pour les vêtements n'est pas

....

[5]

Exercise 2

Now you will hear Angélique talking about her search for work. You will hear this twice.

Answer the questions in English.

1 When Angélique was at school, where was she sent on work experience? ....

2 What did she like about her temporary job at the hospital? ....

3 How did she feel when she left?
i disappointed
ii ....

4 What does she say is the hardest thing about being out of work? ....

[4]

Exercice 3

Vous allez entendre, deux fois, trois jeunes, Cathy, Sylvain et Martine. Ils parlent de l'argent.
Encerclez la bonne réponse.
Regardez l'exemple.

Exemple:

A cause de l'argent, Cathy s'est disputée avec (son copain / son amie / ses parents).

Sylvain

1 Sylvain (ne reçoit jamais d'argent / reçoit de l'argent de temps en temps / reçoit de l'argent régulièrement).

2 Sylvain voudrait (chercher du travail / quitter le foyer / discuter avec ses parents).

Martine

3 Martine est plus (mûre / déprimée / fière) que Cathy et Sylvain.

Justifiez votre résponse.

____

____

____

[6]

Answers

Listening / Foundation

Exercice 1
1 = F; 2 = E; 3 = H + D (either order);
4 = B + A (either order) [6]

Exercice 2
Mylène tick: cycling and swimming
André tick: football and sailing [4]

Exercise 3
1 = C; 2 = B; 3 = A; 4 = C [4]

Exercice 4
1 = C; 2 = G; 3 = E;
4 = A; 5 = F; 6 = D [6]

Listening / Foundation + Higher

Exercise 1
1 = ROCHE
2 = double ✓; bathroom ✓
3 = 9th to 13th of July
4 = balcony + room on 1st floor [4]

Exercice 2
lundi = maillot
mardi = mairie + 18h 30
mercredi = disco (dancer)
jeudi = l'argent; la poste (devant)
vendredi = tour du château + acheter des souvenirs;
pique-nique
samedi = aéroport [10] (1 mark for each item)

Exercice 3
1 = B; 2 = B; 3 = C; 4 = C; 5 = A;
6 = C [6]

Listening / Higher

Exercice 1
1 glisser/aller vite
2 le mercredi et le week-end
3 plus facile que le surf
4 savoir nager
5 intéressante [5]

Exercise 2
1 In a retirement home.
2 The atmosphere was good.
3 Not surprised.
4 Staying idle / inactive or not doing anything. [4]

Exercice 3
Sylvain
1 reçoit de l'argent de temps en temps = 2
2 chercher du travail = 2
Martine
3 mûre = 1
Elle a négocié avec ses parents = 1 [6]

TOTALS: Foundation + Foundation / Higher = 40
Foundation / Higher + Higher = 35

Speaking F

Give yourself 15 minutes to prepare the two role play activities.

Candidate's role: You are in a French café, ordering a snack. Your teacher will play the part of the waiter / waitress and will start the conversation.

	Teacher
1  Say you would like a snack. (e.g. chips)	Mademoiselle.
2  Ask if there are any sandwiches.	Voilà et avec ça?
	Oui nous en avons au fromage, au jambon et au pâté.
3  Say what kind of sandwich you would like.	
4  Ask for a cold drink and a hot drink.	D'accord et comme boisson?
5  Ask where the toilets are.	Très bien.
	Les toilettes? Elles sont au fond du couloir.

Speaking F/H

Candidate's role: You have lost a sports bag on a train and you go to the lost property office. Your teacher will play the part of the employee and will start the conversation.

	Teacher
	Bonjour je peux vous aider?
1 Greet the employee and say what you have lost.	
	Pouvez-vous me décrire le sac?
2 Describe the bag. (2 details)	
	Où avez-vous perdu le sac?
3 Reply to the question.	
	A quelle heure?
4 Say when you lost the bag.	
	D'accord. Et qu'est-ce qu'il y avait dans le sac?
5 Describe what was in the bag. (2 details)	
	Bon, je vais voir si on l'a trouvé.

Speaking H

EITHER (Edexcel type)

You see this advertisement for a job on a children's summer camp and ring up to give details about yourself. You have some experience of this kind of work.

COLONIE DE VACANCES
ETE 98
RECHERCHE
MONITEURS/MONITRICES

BON NIVEAU EN ANGLAIS
ET FRANCAIS

Teacher's questions
1 Pouvez-vous me donner vos détails personnels. Nom? Age? Nationalité?
2 Parlez-vous des langues étrangères? – couramment?
3 Quelle expérience avez-vous de ce travail? Où? Quand?
4 Quand pouvez-vous travailler?

OR (OCR type)

Situation: The notes and pictures below give an outline of one day last year on a visit to Belgium.

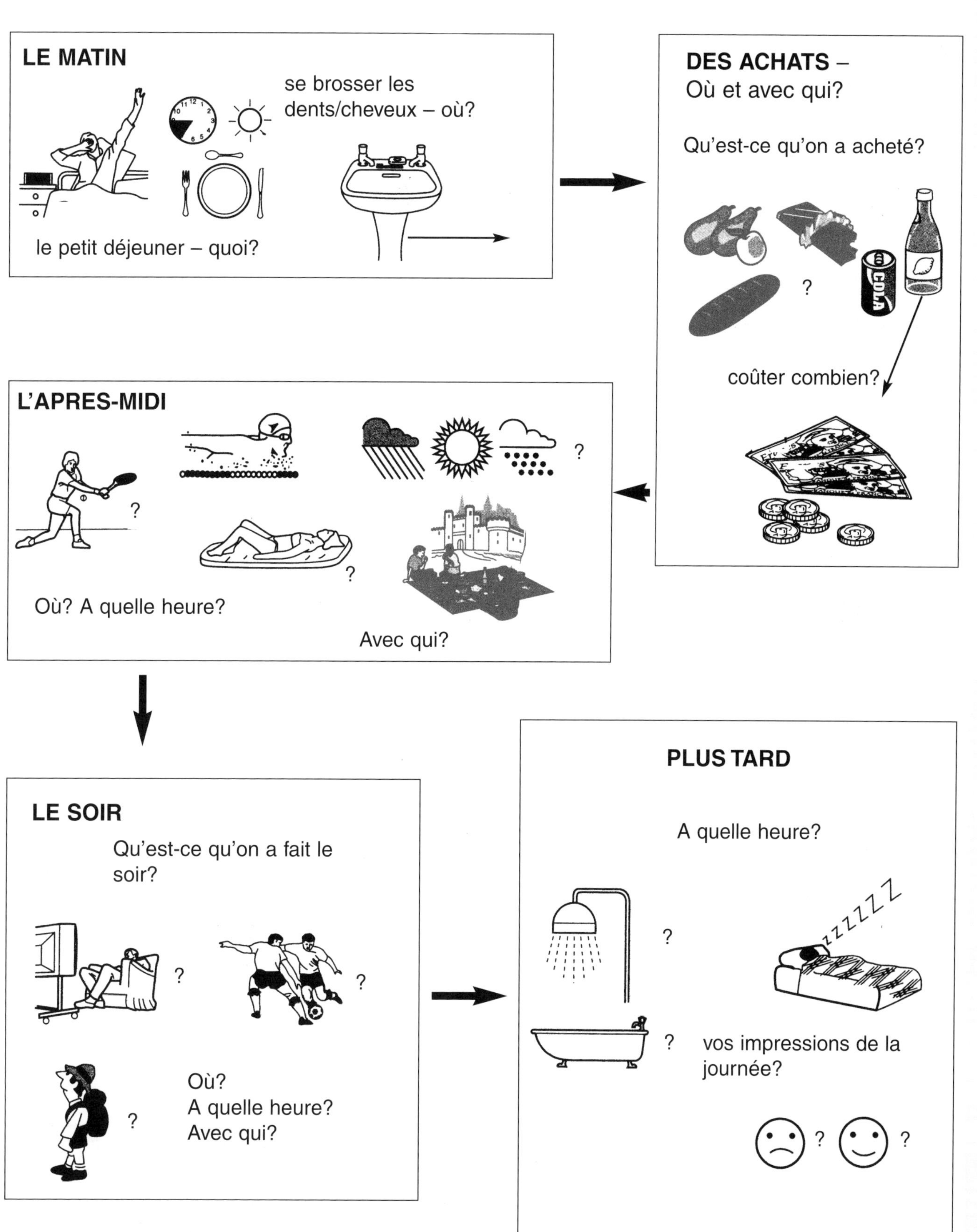

Answers

Speaking / Foundation

1 Je voudrais une portion de frites / des frites.
2 Avez-vous des sandwichs?
3 Je voudrais un sandwich au jambon.
4 Je voudrais une limonade et un café.
5 Est-ce qu il y a des toilettes? / Où sont les toilettes?

Speaking / Foundation + Higher

1 J'ai perdu un sac de sports.
2 Il est / (+ colour such as noir / marron / bleu) (+ size such as grand / petit – other details acceptable).
3 J'ai perdu le sac dans un train.
4 J'ai perdu le sac à (+ time).
5 Il y avait (+ two details such as mon appareil / des vêtements / un porte-feuille).

Speaking / Higher

1 Je m'appelle .... J'ai ... ans. Je suis anglais(e).
2 Je parle anglais et français (allemand / espagnol) couramment / depuis cinq ans.
3 J'ai travaillé dans une colonie en Angleterre l'année dernière (other places / dates acceptable). Be prepared to give extra appropriate details!
4 Je peux / pourrai travailler du (+ date) au (+ date).

OR

L'année dernière j'ai fait un séjour en Belgique. Le matin je me suis levé(e) à 8 heures et je suis descendu(e) dans la cuisine où j'ai pris mon petit déjeuner – j'ai mangé du pain et j'ai bu du café. Après ça, je me suis brossé les dents et les cheveux. Après, on a décidé de faire un pique-nique alors je suis allé(e) au supermarché avec mon ami. On a acheté du pain, du jambon, du fromage et des tomates. Pour boire on a choisi de la limonade puis on a payé – c'était 8 euros 50. Après avoir fait les achats on a fait un pique-nique près du château. On a nagé et après le pique-nique, on a joué au tennis puis on s'est bronzé parce qu'il faisait très beau et très chaud. Vers 6 heures on est rentré. On a regardé un peu de télévision puis j'ai joué au foot et j'ai fait une promenade avec des copains. Je suis rentré(e) vers 8 heures. J'ai pris le dîner et après, je me suis lavé(e) et je me suis couché(e) parce que j'étais très fatigué(e). J'ai passé une très bonne journée – c'était génial – je me suis bien amusé(e).

Reading F

Exercice 1 On fait du shopping!

Choisissez le bon magasin (A – H).

Ecrivez la bonne lettre.

Exemple:

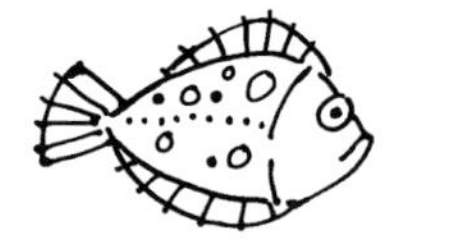

= C

1  = __

2   = __

3 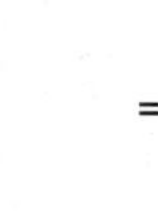

= __

4  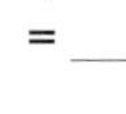 = __

5  = __

6 

= __

Magasins

A BOULANGERIE
B PATISSERIE
C ~~POISSONNERIE~~ (exemple)
D TABAC
E EPICERIE
F CHARCUTERIE
G PHARMACIE
H LIBRAIRIE
I BIJOUTERIE
J BOUCHERIE [6]

Exercice 2 On fait du sport!

Cochez la bonne case.

Exemple:

dimanche = A ☑ B ☐ C ☐

Centre Aéré de Brignais

Programme:	dimanche	tournoi de tennis
	lundi	planche à voile
	mardi	stage de vélo
	mercredi	tournoi de pêche
	jeudi	promenade à cheval
	vendredi	stage de voile
	samedi	natation

1 lundi = A ☐ B ☐ C ☐

2 mardi = A ☐ B ☐ C ☐

3 mercredi = A ☐ B ☐ C ☐

4 jeudi = A ☐ B ☐ C ☐

5 vendredi = A ☐ B ☐ C ☐

6 samedi = A ☐ B ☐ C ☐

[6]

Exercise 3

Answer the questions in English.

CIRQUE PINDER

du 2 août – 16 août

- Achetez deux places et la troisième place est **gratuite**!
- Présentez-vous aux caisses du cirque avec ce papier avant 17 heures.

Horaires des séances d'été.
Matinée 18h (après la plage).
Soirée 21h 15.
Prix des places à partir de 8€.

1 What do you get if you buy two circus tickets?

2 What should you take with you to get the special offer?

3 By what time do you have to arrive at the ticket office?

4 What does the leaflet suggest that you might do **before** you go to a matinée performance?

[4]

Exercice 4

CAMP DU SOLEIL

- Un camping superbe et moderne.
- Situé à 5 minutes d'une plage splendide.
- 150 emplacements spacieux pour tentes et caravanes.
- Jeux pour enfants.
- Magasin d'alimentation ouvert tous les jours.
- Plats cuisinés à emporter.
- Ouvert de juin à octobre.

(Les animaux sont interdits)

caravanes
enfants
fermé
loin
ouvert
près
provisions
venir
interdit
~~**l'internet**~~

Complétez chaque phrase avec UN mot choisi dans cette liste.

Exemple: On peut regarder cette publicité sur ....l'internet.... .

a Ce camping est situé .... de la plage.

b Il y a beaucoup de place pour les tentes et les ....

c Le camping est .... à Pâques.

d On peut acheter des .... au camping.

[4]

Reading F/H

Exercice 1

Lisez ces renseignements touristiques.

A

Les P'tits Mousses – Jeux
Club de Plage (2 – 10 ans)
Ouvert le 1er juillet
au 21 août

B

Cave Jean-Guy et
Bruno Arrivé
Pineau des Charentes
– Vins Fins

C

AVIS IMMOBILIER
2 rue Gaulté – St Gilles
Transactions immobilières –
locations

D

L'ami du Pêcheur
juillet Promenade en mer
mardi et jeudi –
Port de Croix-de-Vie

E

MARCHÉ ARTISANAL
NOCTURNE
Place du Vieux Port
Pensez à vos cadeaux!

F

Promenade Pédestre
Visite guidée des ports
de pêche et de plaisance
Inscription à l'Office de
Tourisme

G

Fête du 14 juillet
St Gilles Croix-de-Vie
défilé, bal populaire,
feux d'artifice à 22 h

H

Vivre le Moyen Age:
8 – 25 août
Au Château de Talmont
monument historique

Ecrivez la bonne lettre.

Exemple: Mon père veut déguster le vin. ....B........

1 Je voudrais me promener et visiter les quais. ....
2 Mon ami veut louer un appartement. ....
3 Mon petit frère veut jouer et s'amuser. ....
4 Je voudrais danser et voir un spectacle. ....
5 Je voudrais me promener en bateau. ....
6 Ma mère veut acheter des souvenirs ce soir. ....

[6]

Exercice 2

Lisez cette lettre.

Toulon
le 6 septembre

Chère Axelle,

J'espère que tu as passé de bonnes vacances à Biarritz; j'ai reçu ta carte – merci! Moi, j'ai passé le mois de juillet à travailler comme serveuse dans un café. C'était amusant, mais fatigant. Quand je ne travaillais pas je sortais avec mes copains. Le soir on allait en boîte et on se promenait dans le port – c'était chouette.

En août je suis allée chez ma correspondante espagnole. On s'entendait assez bien, elle est sympa, mais j'ai eu du mal à comprendre la famille, surtout le frère qui parlait vite. En plus j'ai trouvé qu'on mange très tard, le soir, en Espagne – j'avais toujours faim. On a visité Barcelone et j'ai adoré la ville mais le voyage pour y aller était long!

Demain, c'est la rentrée – je passe en première, j'aurai du travail à faire cette année!

Ecris-moi vite.

Sandrine

Cochez la case Vrai si l'affirmation est vraie.
Cochez la case Faux si l'affirmation est fausse et corrigez l'affirmation en français.

	Vrai	Faux
Exemple: Axelle a passé ses vacances à Paris.	☐	☑
Axelle a passé ses vacances à Biarritz.		
1 Sandrine est partie en vacances en juillet.	☐	☐
2 Elle a travaillé à la caisse d'un café.	☐	☐
3 En juillet, Sandrine est allée danser.	☐	☐
4 Elle ne comprenait pas le frère de sa correspondante.	☐	☐
5 Elle avait faim en Espagne parce qu'elle n'aimait pas la nourriture.	☐	☐
6 Sandrine est rentrée en France pour travailler.	☐	☐

[10]

Exercise 3

Read this article and answer the questions in English.

Plus d'école l'après-midi

Matières scolaires le matin, sport et activités culturelles l'après-midi ....; à la prochaine rentrée scolaire, plus de 200 villes testeront ces nouveaux rythmes scolaires. L'objectif est de permettre aux enfants de s'épanouir davantage mais aussi d'aménager des journées moins fatigantes. Les établissements scolaires concernés sont surtout des écoles primaires. Mais des collèges participeront aussi à l'expérience. Si ça marche, peut-être qu'un jour toutes les écoles adopteront ces nouvelles journées.

1 From next September, what will some pupils be doing in the afternoons?

i .... ii ....

2 How many towns will take part in the experiment?

....

3 One of the aims of this experiment is (choose one):

A ☐ to make the school day less tiring.

B ☐ to close the schools at lunchtime.

C ☐ to employ fewer teaching staff.

4 Most of the schools in this experiment are

.... [4]

Reading H

Exercise 1

Read this letter to a magazine.
Answer the questions in English.

Mes parents

Je trouve mes parents assez cools. Seulement, j'ai toujours peur de les décevoir alors je dois parfois mentir. Je sais qu'ils s'inquiètent beaucoup pour moi car je suis restée longtemps sans copines. Depuis que je suis au collège ça va mieux mais j'ai souvent le blues. Ma mère est accro aux notes du collège et mon père veut que je réussisse dans la musique. Ils se disputent souvent, disant que soit la musique soit l'école est le plus important. Moi, je suis coincée car il faudrait que je réussisse partout sinon l'un des deux est sur mon dos jusqu'aux prochaines vacances. (Clotilde – 15 ans)

1 Why does Clotilde feel that she sometimes has to lie to her parents?

2 What made her parents worry about her when she was at junior school?

3 Why do Clotilde's parents argue?

4 How does Clotilde feel about the present situation? [4]

Exercice 2

Lisez cet article.

La natation synchronisée

Marianne Aeschbacher est une des championnes françaises les plus titrées .... Aujourd'hui, elle prépare les Jeux Olympiques ....

Okapi: A quel âge avez-vous commencé à pratiquer la natation synchronisée?

Marianne: A 9 ans. Je faisais de la danse classique et de la natation sportive. Comme je ne pouvais plus faire les deux, j'ai choisi un sport qui alliait les deux disciplines. En natation synchronisée, il vaut mieux commencer tôt et il faut être patient, car ce sport demande beaucoup d'efforts.

Okapi: Tout en menant votre carrière sportive vous n'avez jamais délaissé les études ....

Marianne: Il faut préparer sa sortie du sport. C'est une question d'équilibre aussi. Quand ça ne marche pas sur le plan sportif, ça permet de prendre du recul.

Okapi: Vous arrêtez votre carrière après les Jeux Olympiques. N'est-ce pas trop dur d'admettre qu'à 25 ans, pour ce sport, on est déjà vieille.

Marianne: Si, bien sûr. Mais, j'ai des souvenirs formidables, j'ai fait de superbes voyages. Mais l'essentiel c'est de ne jamais oublier que ce qui compte avant tout, c'est de se faire plaisir bien plus que les résultats.

Cochez la bonne case.

1 Pourquoi Marianne a-t-elle choisi de faire de la natation synchronisée?

Elle n'arrivait pas à nager très rapidement. A ☐
Elle voulait combiner ses deux sports préférés. B ☐
Elle ne voulait plus faire de danse classique. C ☐

2 Il vaut mieux commencer ce sport tôt car . . .

il faut du temps pour réussir. A ☐
il faut être petite de taille. B ☐
il faut être souple. C ☐

3 Que dit-elle à propos de son mode de vie?

Elle a laissé tomber ses études. A ☐
Le sport est la chose la plus importante dans sa vie. B ☐
Il faut qu'elle pense à son avenir. C ☐

4 Comment Marianne a-t-elle profité de ses expériences?

Elle a rencontré beaucoup de jeunes. A ☐
Elle a eu de bons résultats. B ☐
Elle s'est bien amusée. C ☐

[4]

Exercice 3

Lisez le texte.

Strasbourg:

Le royaume des piétons

Depuis lundi 24 février 6 h 30 du matin, les voitures n'ont plus le droit de traverser le centre-ville de Strasbourg (Alsace). Celui-ci est devenu le royaume des piétons, des vélos et des bus. Cela fait quinze ans que Strasbourg prévoit de créer un centre-ville réservé aux piétons. Ce plan s'appelle "Strass" et a pour but de réduire (diminuer) la pollution et les embouteillages (les bouchons de voitures). Depuis le lundi 24 février, les voitures ne peuvent plus traverser le centre-ville. Elles doivent prendre des périphériques (routes extérieures au centre-ville).

Résultat: le centre-ville de Strasbourg ressemblait ce lundi à un lundi du mois d'août. Seuls les piétons, les cyclistes et les bus circulaient dans les rues du centre-ville. Strasbourg est la première grande ville française à fermer son centre-ville aux voitures. Après avoir été la première à obliger les voitures à ne pas dépasser les 50km/h, Strasbourg veut aujourd'hui changer les habitudes des gens et les pousser à utiliser les transports en commun (bus, tramway...).

Ce système est déjà testé avec succès en Allemagne et aux Pays-Bas. Catherine Trautmann, le maire de Strasbourg, veut "rendre la ville aux Strasbourgeois". Mais cela ne plaît pas à tout le monde. Les commerçants du centre-ville protestent. Ils pensent qu'ils auront beaucoup moins de clients. L'expérience de Strasbourg, si elle réussit, va sûrement donner envie aux autres villes françaises de faire la même chose. Toutes souffrent de la pollution et du trop grand nombre de voitures.

Répondez en **français** aux questions.

Exemple: Depuis quand les voitures n'ont-elles plus le droit de traverser le centre-ville?

Lundi 24 février

a Quels véhicules peuvent traverser le centre-ville de Strasbourg?

....

....

b Quelle est l'idée de plan "Strass"?

....

c Les voitures, où passent-elles maintenant?

....

d Qui est Catherine Trautmann?

....

e Qui n'est pas content du nouveau plan?

....

[6]

Exercice 4

Lisez cet article.

Qu'avez-vous fait de vos 15 ans?

Françoise Giroud, Ancien ministre, journaliste

A 15 ans, je travaillais déjà depuis un an. J'étais sténo-dactylo et vendeuse dans une librairie. Je n'avais pas le choix. Ma mère avait été ruinée par la mort de mon père, j'ai donc dû quitter l'école. C'était très difficile, mais à 15 ans, on a du ressort.

J'avais passé trois mois dans une école pour apprendre la dactylo, je ne voulais pas rester vendeuse toute ma vie..... Je ne rêvais d'aucun métier précis, j'avais depuis longtemps renoncé à mon désir d'être médecin, les études coûtant bien trop chères. Il y avait tout de même un avantage à travailler dans une librairie: J'ai lu tout le magasin, de Balzac à Tolstoï, par ordre alphabétique!

Mes distractions étaient réduites au minimum. J'étais très solitaire. Ma soeur aînée me tenait lieu d'amie. Quant aux garçons, je ne m'y intéressais pas, à une exception près: j'étais amoureuse depuis l'âge de 10 ans du réalisateur Marc Allégret, qui était un ami de ma famille. C'est aussi grâce à lui que l'année suivante, j'ai quitté la librairie, en devenant scripte pour un de ses films.

Répondez aux questions **en français.**

1 A quel âge Françoise a-t-elle commencé à travailler?

....

2 Pourquoi a-t-elle dû quitter l'école?

....

3 Pourquoi a-t-elle appris la dactylo?

....

4 Pourquoi n'est-elle pas devenue médecin?

....

5 Quel était son passe-temps préféré?

....

6 En parlant de ses distractions elle dit qu'elle (cochez une case).

A ☐ avait peu d'amies.
B ☐ sortait souvent avec des garçons.
C ☐ ne s'entendait pas avec les garçons.
D ☐ ne s'entendait pas avec sa soeur.

7 Après avoir travaillé à la librairie, qu'est-ce qu'elle a fait?

....

[7]

Writing F

Exercice 1

You are booking for a penfriend.

Fill in the form **in French**. [10]

Nom: 1

Nationalité: 1

Date de naissance: le .... mois 19 1

Sport préféré: 1

Autres passe-temps: i 1

ii 1

Plat préféré: 1

Boisson préférée: 1

Couleur des cheveux: 1

Matières d'école préférées: i..1

ii 1

Exercice 2

You are on holiday.

Write a postcard to your friend.

Say:

- where you are (e.g. France, region of England)
- who you are with
- where you are staying (e.g. campsite, hotel)
- what you are doing (2 details) [10]

Writing F/H

Exercice 1

Your French friend Axelle has written to you.

Write a reply to her. Answer all her questions.

Torreilles

le 9 septembre

Salut!

Ça va? J'espère que tu as passé de bonnes vacances. Qu'est-ce que tu as fait, et avec qui? Est-ce que tu as travaillé pendant les vacances – moi, j'ai eu de la chance et j'ai trouvé du travail dans un café. Quels sont tes projets pour Noël? Ma mère voudrait t'inviter à passer 15 jours ici chez nous. Qu'en penses-tu?

Réponds-moi vite!

Ton amie,

Axelle

[20]

Answers

Reading / Foundation

Exercice 1

1 = A; **2** = I; **3** = E; **4** = F; **5** = B; **6** = G [6]

Exercice 2

1 = B; **2** = A; **3** = A; **4** = C; **5** = B; **6** = B [6]

Exercise 3

1 3rd ticket free

2 This piece of paper / leaflet

3 Before 17h (5 pm)

4 Go to the beach [4]

Exercice 4

a = près; **b** = caravanes;
c = fermé; **d**= provisions [4]

TOTAL = [20]

Reading / Foundation + Higher

Exercice 1

1 = F; **2** = C; **3** = A; **4** = G; **5** = D; **6** = E [6]

Exercice 2

1 Faux. Elle a travaillé en juillet or Elle est partie en août.

2 Faux. Elle a travaillé comme serveuse.

3 Vrai. **4** Vrai.

5 Faux. On mange très tard en Espagne.

6 Faux. Elle est rentrée pour aller à l'école/ or c'est la rentrée scolaire. [10]

Exercise 3

1 i sports / ii cultural activities

2 More than 200

3 A

4 Primary / Junior schools [4]

TOTAL = [20]

Reading / Higher

Exercise 1

1 So that she won't disappoint them/let them down.

2 She had no friends.

3 One says (father) that music is more important, the other that her school work is more important.

4 She feels trapped/caught between the two of them, has to do well in everything. [4]

Exercice 2

1 = B; **2** = A; **3** = C; **4** = C [4]

Exercice 3

a voitures + bus + vélos OR bus + car or tram (any 1 of 3 = 1 mark); **b** réduire/baisser la pollution; **c** routes extérieures/périfériques; **d** le maire; **e** les commerçants. [5]

Exercice 4

1 14 ans **2** Son père est mort/Pour gagner de l'argent. **3** Elle ne voulait pas rester vendeuse toute sa vie. **4** Les études étaient/coûtaient trop chères. **5** la lecture/lire **6** a **7** Elle a travaillé comme scripte pour Marc Allégret *not* elle a toumé un film. [7]

TOTAL = [20]

Writing H

Exercice 1

Vous voyez un débat dans un magazine.

Débat

Que pensez-vous de votre ville / village?
Participez à notre débat.
Ecrivez vos réponses à nos questions.

- Où habitez-vous?
- Décrivez les avantages d'habiter votre ville/village.
- Décrivez les inconvénients de votre ville/village.
- Aimez-vous habiter votre ville/village? Pourquoi/pas?

Ecrivez une réponse au magazine (150 mots maximum).

[20]

Answers

Writing / Foundation

Exercice 1

anglais / anglaise / le + date (figures acceptable) janvier, etc. :

le tennis / foot / badminton / rugby, etc. – accept any sport / accept the name of any other pastimes such as (la) danse / danser, vélo / faire du vélo, lecture / lire, etc:

plat préfére – accept any main course such as la viande, le poisson, le poulet / boisson préférée – accept any drink, le café / le thé / le coca, etc:

couleur des cheveux – any sensible colour acceptable!:

any two school subjects acceptable.

Each item = 1 if the message is put across – the spelling does not have to be perfect but recognisable!

10 x 1 = [10]

Exercice 2

- Je suis à + name / en France / au bord de la mer.
- avec ma famille / mes amis.
- Je reste / séjourne à l'hôtel / dans un camping, etc.
- Je nage et je joue au volley.

Amitiés ....

Each task successfully completed (message understood fully) = 2

5 x 2 = [10]

Writing / Foundation + Higher

Differerent exam awarding bodies have different ways of marking at this level. Basically between one-third and one half of the marks are available for Communication (i.e. answering the set tasks / questions in the letter) and the remaining marks are rewarded for the accuracy of the language you use and the way you use it.

Here is a model answer.

Chère Axelle,

Merci bien de ta lettre. Moi, aussi, j'ai passé de bonnes vacances. Je suis allée dans la région des lacs avec mes amis. On est resté dans des auberges de jeunesse. Je me suis promenée à la montagne et j'ai nagé dans les lacs. C'était chouette. Après mon séjour à Windermere j'ai travaillé dans un magasin près de chez moi.

J'aimerais beaucoup passer les vacances de Noël chez toi et je te remercie de l'invitation. Je pourrai venir du 20 décembre au 4 janvier. Ça va? Moi, j'attends les vacances avec impatience!

Ecris-moi vite

Caroline

Writing / Higher

Again, different exam awarding bodies mark the final question on the Higher Writing Paper in slightly different ways. Some marks are available for Communication but more are rewarded for the accuracy of the language you use and the way you use it. Try to be as accurate as possible if you want to gain high marks.

Here is a model answer.

Mon village

J'habite à la campagne dans un petit village pittoresque dans le sud-ouest de l'Angleterre à 20 km de la ville de Bath. Il y a deux mille habitants dans le village. Je trouve le paysage autour du village agréable. C'est une région rurale et agricole et j'aime habiter ici parce que c'est tranquille et il n'y a pas beaucoup de pollution.

J'ai beaucoup d'amis dans le village. On fait du vélo et on va souvent faire du shopping à Bath. Il y a souvent beaucoup de touristes à Bath car c'est une ville très historique avec beaucoup de monuments à visiter. On peut aussi aller au cinéma et au théâtre à Bath.

Il y a quand même des inconvénients pour les jeunes. Le soir, il n'y a rien à faire (il faut un club des jeunes) et la boîte la plus près est à dix kilomètres. Alors il est difficile de rentrer si on sort en boîte ou à Bath parce que les bus s'arrêtent à 8h du soir!

J'aime habiter ici mais il n'y a pas assez de distractions pour les jeunes.

Grammar

Whether you are going to sit Foundation or Higher papers (or a mix of both), you will not only need to learn the vocabulary in the earlier chapters but also the grammatical rules which make French work. Some of the sections are marked **Active** which means you should be able to produce the structures (e.g. in Speaking and Writing). Other sections are marked **Receptive** which means you only need to recognise and understand them (e.g. in Reading and Listening). Sections are also marked F (Foundation) or H (Higher). If you are entered for the Foundation Tier, miss out the sections marked H Receptive and H Active.

Verbs

1	Present tense	F + H Active
2	Perfect tense	F + H Active
3	Imperfect tense	F Receptive / H Active
4	Future tense (and near Future)	F + H Active
5	Pluperfect tense	H Active
6	Past historic tense	H Receptive
7	Conditional tense	F Receptive / H Active
8	Conditional perfect tense	H Receptive
9	Venir de + infinitive	F + H Active
10	Present subjunctive	H Receptive
11	Present participle	F Receptive / H Active
12	Infinitives (using two verbs together)	F Receptive / H Active
13	Perfect infinitive	F Receptive / H Active
14	Negatives	F + H Active
15	Imperatives (giving orders)	F Receptive / H Active
16	Interrogatives (how to ask questions)	F + H Active
17	Passive voice	H Receptive

Nouns

1	Gender	F + H Active
2	Definite article	F + H Active
3	Indefinite article	F + H Active
4	Partitive article	F + H Active
5	Plurals	F + H Active
6	Possession	F + H Active

Adjectives

1	Formation and position	F + H Active
2	Possessive adjectives	F + H Active
3	Demonstrative adjectives	F Receptive / H Active
4	Comparative and superlative adjectives	F + H Active
5	Indefinite adjectives	F + H Active

Adverbs

1	Formation	F + H Active
2	Comparatives and superlatives	F + H Active

Pronouns

1	Subject pronouns	F + H Active
2	Direct object pronouns	F + H Active
3	Indirect object pronouns	F + H Active
4	En	F + H Active
5	Y	F + H Active
6	Position of pronouns	F Receptive / H Active
7	Emphatic pronouns	F + H Active
8	Relative pronouns	F + H Active
9	Interrogative pronouns	F + H Active
10	Demonstrative pronouns	F + H Active
11	Possessive pronouns	H Receptive
12	Indefinite pronouns	F + H Active

Verbs

The most important part of a sentence is the verb. It is a word which shows an action. Dictionaries list verbs by the present infinitive forms, such as manger = to eat.

There are three main groups of French verbs related to the last two letters of the present infinitive.

- Group 1 **er** (such as donn**er**)
- Group 2 **ir** (such as fin**ir**)
- Group 3 **re** (such as vend**re**)

Remove the last two letters of the infinitive to get the 'stem' of the verb.

Infinitive – regarder: regard = stem

You need the stems of the verbs in the three groups to form the different tenses (using time zones); these will help you talk about past, present and future events. You also need the stem of the verb so that you can add the appropriate ending for the subject of the verb or the person performing the action.

Remember, if you are using the person's name (Paul or Anne) use the part of the verb that goes with il or elle. For more than one person (Paul and Anne) use the part of the verb that goes with ils.

Irregular verbs, those that don't follow any of the patterns of the three main groups, are listed under each tense.

1 Present Tense

When is it used?

To talk about an action happening now or which happens normally: such as I eat at 6 o'clock or I am eating = je mange.

- Group 1 **-er** verbs, such as donner
  Add -e, -es, -e, -ons, -ez or -ent to the stem.

For example:

je donn**e**	= I give / am giving
tu donn**es**	= you give / are giving
il / elle / on donn**e**	= he / she / one gives / is giving
nous donn**ons**	= we give / are giving
vous donn**ez**	= you give / are giving
ils / elles donn**ent**	= they give / are giving

- Group 2 **-ir** verbs, such as finir
  Add -is, -is, -it, -issons, -issez or -issent to the stem.

je fin**is** = I finish / am finishing
tu fin**is**
il / elle / on fin**it**
nous fin**issons**
vous fin**issez**
ils / elles fin**issent**

- Group 3 **-re** verbs, such as vendre
  Add s, -s, __, -ons, -ez or -ent to the stem.

je vend**s** = I sell / am selling
tu vend**s**
il / elle / on vend
nous vend**ons**
vous vend**ez**
ils / elles vend**ent**

Important irregular verbs. Look up the infinitive in a dictionary if you are unsure about the meaning.

APPELER = to call
j'appelle tu appelles il / elle / on appelle nous appelons vous appelez ils / elles appellent

AVOIR = to have
j'ai tu as il / elle / on a nous avons vous avez ils / elles ont

ETRE = to be
je suis tu es il / elle / on est nous sommes vous êtes ils / elles sont

COURIR = to run
je cours tu cours il / elle / on court nous courons vous courez ils / elles courent

DORMIR = to sleep
je dors tu dors il / elle / on dort nous dormons vous dormez ils / elles dorment

FAIRE = to do, make
je fais tu fais il / elle / on fait nous faisons vous faites ils / elles font

LIRE = to read
je lis tu lis il / elle lit nous lisons vous lisez ils / elles lisent

METTRE = to put
je mets tu mets il / elle / on met Nous mettons vous mettez ils / elles mettent

VENIR = to come
je viens tu viens il / elle on vient nous venons vous venez ils / elles viennent

Reflexive verbs

A reflexive action is an action done to oneself.

se laver = to wash (oneself)

je me lave
tu te laves
il / elle / on se lave
nous nous lavons
vous vous lavez
ils / elles se lavent

Present tense + depuis

Je mange depuis une heure.	= I have been eating for an hour.
Je regarde la télévision depuis dix minutes.	= I have been watching television for ten minutes.

2 Perfect Tense

Going for a C?

You should be confident about using this tense; make the most of the word lists on pages 86, 91 and 109.

When is it used?

To describe a finished action (in the past), e.g.
I got up, I ate breakfast, I went to school.

All verbs need:

a a helper (auxiliary) verb.
This is part of avoir or être in the present, such as j'ai / je suis.

b a past participle (see below).

Revise the verbs avoir and être (present tense).

Which auxiliary verb: avoir or être?

Nearly all of them take avoir!
But here's an easy way to remember the verbs that are formed with être; use the mnemonic MR VANS TRAMPED!

M	monter	= to go up
R	rester	= to stay
V	venir (also revenir)	= to come (back)
A	aller	= to go
N	naître	= to be born
S	sortir	= to go out
T	tomber	= to fall
R	retourner	= to return
A	arriver	= to arrive
M	mourir	= to die
P	partir	= to leave
E	entrer (also rentrer)	= to go (back) in
D	descendre	= to go down

How does it work?

Choose the correct part of avoir or être to go with the subject, such as j'ai or je suis. Then you need the past participle.

How do I get the past participle?

- Group 1 verbs -er (donner)
  add é   to the stem   (donné*)
- Group 2 verbs -ir (finir)
  add i   to the stem   (fini)
- Group 3 verbs -re (vendre)
  add u   to the stem   (vendu)

* You should *never* forget this accent on the é – it's very important, without it, the meaning can change.

Now put the two together:

j'ai mangé = I ate
j'ai regardé = I watched

With avoir, past participles don't agree with the person performing the action (so don't add -e, -s or -es). For preceding direct object agreements – see Pronouns 2 (on page 138). However, with être, past participles do agree.

How does the past participle agree?

Once you know which verbs take être, it gets easier! Remember MR VANS TRAMPED.

a use the correct form of être, such as je suis.

b form the past participle using the above rules:

find the stem	**add the correct ending**
aller – all	allé (past participle)
sortir – sort	sorti
descendre – descend	descendu

Example: je suis allé = I went (m)
je suis allée = I went (f)

Watch out for these exceptions!
mourir: **mort**
naître: **né**
venir: **venu**

BEWARE you must make être past participles agree with the gender of the person performing the action ...

FEMALE	**MALE**
je suis allé**e** (add an -e)	je suis allé (nothing added)
tu es allé**e**	tu es allé
elle est allé**e**	il est allé

... and with the number of people performing the action.

PLURAL FEMININE	**PLURAL MASCULINE**
nous sommes allé**es**	nous sommes all**és**
vous êtes allé**es**	vous êtes all**és**
elles sont allé**es**	ils sont all**és**

Remember:
MR VANS TRAMPED past participles agree!

Most irregular verbs use avoir as the auxiliary.
Learn the past participles carefully!

avoir: j'ai eu	= I had
boire: j'ai bu	= I drank
conduire: j'ai conduit	= I drove
dire: j'ai dit	= I said
écrire: j'ai écrit	= I wrote
être: j'ai été	= I have been
faire: j'ai fait	= I did / I made
lire: j'ai lu	= I read
mettre: j'ai mis	= I put
ouvrir: j'ai ouvert	= I opened
prendre: j'ai pris	= I took
savoir: j'ai su	= I know
voir: j'ai vu	= I saw
vouloir: j'ai voulu	= I wanted

Reflexive verbs use être as the auxiliary.

je me suis levé(e) = I got up
tu t'es levé(e)
il s'est levé
elle s'est levée
nous nous sommes levé(e)s
vous vous êtes levé(e)s
ils se sont levés
elles se sont levées

3 Imperfect Tense

Some exam awarding bodies require you to produce this tense in the Speaking and Writing skills as well as recognise it if you are Going for a C. The imperfect, also a past tense, describes **un**finished actions whereas the perfect tense describes finished actions.

Here's a summary of the main uses of the imperfect tense:

i to describe something which used to happen regularly or repeatedly.

J'**allais** au cinéma tous les vendredis.	= I used to go to the cinema on Fridays.

ii to describe something which was happening (imperfect) when something else happened (perfect).

Je **regardais** la télévision quand ma mère est entrée dans la pièce.	= I was watching TV when my mother came into the room.

iii to describe people, weather or things in the past.

Le château **était** beau.	= The castle was beautiful.
J'**étais** content(e) / triste.	= I was happy / sad.
Quand je me suis levé(e), il **faisait** soleil.	= When I got up, it was sunny.

Here's a clue! If the English = 'was + ing', such as I was watching TV, use the imperfect tense of the verb which has 'ing'.

Je regardais.	= I was watching.

How do I form the imperfect?

a take the nous form of the present tense. Then remove the -ons.

donner – nous donnons: donn

finir – nous finissons: finiss

vendre – nous vendons: vend

b add the following endings -ais, -ais, -ait, -ions, -iez, or -aient.

je donnais	nous donnions
tu donnais	vous donniez
il / elle / on donnait	ils / elles donnaient

Note this important irregular verb: être

j'étais	tu étais	il était
nous étions	vous étiez	ils étaient

il y avait = there was / there were

Il y avait beaucoup de monde. = There were a lot of people.

C'était chouette! = It was great!

C'était fermé. = It was closed.

4 Future Tense

Going for a C or an A?

You should be able to talk and write about events in the future.

How do I form the future?

- Group 1 ER and Group 2 IR verbs
  - **a** take the infinitive, such as donner, finir.
  - **b** add -ai, -as, -a, -ons, -ez or -ont:

je donnerai = I will give
tu donneras
il / elle / on donnera
nous donnerons
vous donnerez
ils / elles donneront

- Group 3 RE verbs
  - **a** remove the -e from the infinitive, then add the endings as above.

Watch out for irregular verbs!

They have unusual stems, but the endings are as above.

acheter: j'achèterai = I will buy	mourir: je mourrai
aller : j'irai = I will go	pleuvoir: il pleuvra = it will rain
appeler: j'appellerai	pouvoir: je pourrai
avoir: j'aurai	recevoir: je recevrai
courir: je courrai	savoir: je saurai
devoir: je devrai	venir: je viendrai
envoyer: j'enverrai	voir: je verrai
être: je serai	vouloir: je voudrai
faire: je ferai	

In English you often use the present tense where the French use the future.

Elle arrivera (future) quand elle sera (future) prête.	= She will arrive (future) when she is (present) ready.

Use the future after quand in such cases.

How can I avoid the 'future'?

Use the 'near future'! This is easy to use and is like the English – I am going to do something.
Use the correct form of aller + an infinitive.

Je vais manger.	= I am going to eat.
Tu vas sortir.	= You are going to go out.
Il / Elle / On va danser.	= He / She / One is going to dance.
Nous allons partir.	= We are going to leave.
Vous allez chanter.	= You are going to sing.
Ils / Elles vont aller au café.	= They are going to go to the café.

5 Pluperfect Tense

Some exam awarding bodies do not require the active use of this tense, but others do if you are aiming for an A or B grade. If you are Going for a C you should at least recognise it. This tense describes what *had* happened before something else happened (perfect).

How do I form the pluperfect?

Use the imperfect tense of:
either
avoir + past participle.

J'avais mangé. = I had eaten.

or
être + past participle.

J'étais partie(e). = I had left.

Here's a helpful clue! Verbs which take être in the perfect (MR VANS TRAMPED) also take être in the pluperfect, and the past participle agrees.

ALLER
j'étais allé(e) = I had gone
tu étais allé(e)
il était allé
elle était allée
nous étions allé(e)s
vous étiez allé(e)s
ils étaient allés
elles étaient allées

DONNER
j'avais donné = I had given
tu avais donné
il avait donné
elle avait donné
nous avions donné
vous aviez donné
ils avaient donné
elles avaient donné

Reflexive verbs take être (as in the perfect).

Je m'étais levé(e). = I had got up.

6 Past Historic Tense

This tense is used in newspaper articles and novels. It is used to write about events in the past (like the perfect), but you won't have to produce it yourself. You might come across it in a reading exercise, so you must be able to recognise it.

Here are the endings.

- Group 1 ER verbs:
  -ai, -as, -a, -âmes, -âtes, -èrent
  For example: je donnai = I gave
- Group 2 IR verbs + Group 3 RE verbs:
  -is, -is, -it, -îmes, -îtes, -irent
  For example: je finis = I finished, je descendis = I went down

Irregular verbs with unusual stems!

je conduisis = I drove
je dis = I said
j'écrivis = I wrote
je fis = I made
je mis = I put
je pris = I took
je ris = I laughed
je vins = I came
je vis = I saw

7 Conditional Tense

This tense describes what **would** happen. You are already familiar with: je voudrais = I would like.

It is often used with an imperfect tense, and si (if).

Si j'avais beaucoup d'argent, **j'irais** en France. = If I had a lot of money, I **would go** to France.

How do I form the conditional?

a Group 1 + 2 verbs take the infinitive, and Group 3 verbs remove the e from the infinitive.
ER verbs, e.g. donner
IR verbs, e.g. finir
RE verbs, e.g. vendr

b add -ais, -ais, -ait, -ions, -iez or -aient:
Je donnerais. = I would give.

Irregular verbs:
Look back at the unusual stems used in the future (on page 130); these are the same for the conditional with the above endings.

ACHETER (infinitive)
j'achèterai (future)
j'achèterais (conditional)

ALLER (infinitive)
j'irai (future)
j'irais (conditional)

Watch out for these!
j'aurais = I would have
je serais = I would be
je ferais = I would do / make
je voudrais = I would like

8 Conditional Perfect Tense

This translates as 'would have' or 'should have' done something. You only have to be able to recognise this in the exam, but if you can use it you will score 'bonus' marks!

How is it formed?

a select an auxiliary verb (avoir or être) as you would for the perfect tense.

b put the auxiliary verb in the conditional.

AVOIR
j'aurais
tu aurais
il aurait
nous aurions
vous auriez
ils auraient

ETRE
je serais
tu serais
il serait
nous serions
vous seriez
ils seraient

c add the past participle. Remember agreements on past participles using être.

MANGER
j'aurais mangé = I would have eaten tu aurais mangé il / elle / on aurait mangé vous auriez mangé ils auraient mangé elles auraient mangé

ALLER
je serais allé(e) = I would have gone tu serais allé(e) il / on serait allé / elle serait allée vous seriez allé(e)(s) ils seraient allés elles seraient allées

9 Venir de + Infinitive

Use the *present* tense of venir + an infinitive.

Je viens de manger.	= I have just eaten.
Je viens de partir.	= I have just left.
Tu viens de finir.	= You have just finished.
Il / Elle vient de sortir.	= He / She has just gone out.
Nous venons de manger.	= We have just eaten.
Vous venez d'arriver.	= You have just arrived.
Ils viennent de finir.	= They have just finished.

This construction can also be used with the imperfect tense of venir + an infinitive:

Je venais (imperfect) de manger.	= I **had** just eaten.
Elle venait de partir.	= She had just left.

10 Present Subjunctive

Going for an A?

Then you just need to be able to recognise this form which is usually close to the present tense.

Il faut que je mange.	= It is necessary that I (should) eat.

Watch out for these irregular forms!

aller: j'aille
avoir: j'aie
boire: je boive
être: je sois
faire: je fasse
pouvoir: je puisse
savoir: je sache

11 Present Participle

This translates as the 'ing' form of English verbs.

allant = going

donnant = giving

BEWARE! Don't use this where all you need is the present tense.

Je vais.	= I am going.

A present participle is not complete in itself and is best used alongside another verb (see examples below).

How do I form it?

a take the nous form of the present tense such as allons, donnons, finissons, vendons.

b remove the -ons ending.

c add -ant:
allant = going
donnant = giving
finissant = finishing
vendant = selling

Watch out for these irregular present participles!
avoir: ayant savoir: sachant être: étant

Étant riche, elle a acheté beaucoup de cadeaux.	= Being rich, she bought lots of presents.
Voyant qu'il était en retard, il s'est dépêché.	= Seeing that he was late, he hurried up.

The present participle is often used with en = by / while / on doing.

En travaillant dur, elle a réussi à ses examens.	= By working hard she passed her exams.
Il a écouté ses CD en faisant ses devoirs.	= He listened to his CDs while doing his homework.
Elle est rentrée en courant.	= She went running home.

12 Infinitives

Some verbs can be followed by another as in English.

J'aime jouer au tennis.	= I like to play (playing) tennis.
Je veux sortir.	= I want to go out.
Je sais nager.	= I know how to swim.

The basic rule is, as in English, if there are two verbs together, the second is the infinitive form.

J'adore aller au cinéma.	= I love going to the cinema.
J'espère y aller.	= I hope to go there.
Il préfère manger du poisson.	= He prefers to eat fish.
Elle déteste écrire des lettres.	= She hates writing letters.

- Some verbs are always followed with **à** before the infinitive; try to learn the following common ones:

aider à: J'aide à faire la vaisselle.	= I help to wash up.

commencer à   inviter à
continuer à   se mettre à
se décider à   passer du temps à
demander à   réussir à
hésiter à

- Other verbs are always followed with **de** before an infinitive; try these:

décider de: J'ai décidé de sortir.	= I decided to go out.

s'arrêter de — offrir de
cesser de — oublier de
décider de — permettre de
dire de — refuser de
essayer de — regretter de
finir de
avoir besoin de — avoir peur de
avoir le droit de — avoir l'intention de

- sans + infinitive = without

Je suis parti(e) **sans dire** 'au revoir'.	= I left **without saying** goodbye.

- pour + infinitive = in order to

Je travaille **pour réussir** à mes examens!	= I am working in order to pass my exams.

Remember don't use pour after attendre, chercher or payer.

J'attends le bus.	= I'm waiting for the bus.
Je cherche mon stylo.	= I'm looking for my pen.

13 Perfect Infinitive

This is the equivalent of 'after having done' something.

Après avoir mangé, je suis parti(e).	= After having eaten, I left.

Notice the subject of the two verbs is the same.

Après avoir regardé la télévision, j'ai fait mes devoirs.	= After having watched (watching) TV, I did my homework.

How do I form it?

a use après + être (if verbs take être in the perfect), or après + avoir (if verbs take avoir in the perfect).

b add the past participle.

c if using an être verb make the past participle agree with the subject (remember: MR VANS TRAMPED verb).

If it's a woman talking:

Après être arrivée, j'ai pris le dîner.	= After I had arrived, I had dinner.

14 Negatives

In French, the negative form of a verb has two parts such as ne ... pas.

The **ne** goes in front of the verb and the **pas** goes after the verb.

Je ne regarde pas la télévision.	= I don't watch TV.
Je n'aime pas les maths.	= I don't like maths.
Je ne me lève pas tôt.	= I don't get up early.

In the perfect tense the ne and pas go either side of the auxiliary verb (avoir or être).

Je n'ai pas mangé.	= I didn't eat.
Je ne suis pas sorti(e).	= I didn't go out.

After a negative and to translate 'any' use de or d' before a noun.

Je n'ai pas d'argent.	= I haven't got any money.

Other useful negatives

ne ... rien = nothing
ne ... jamais = never
ne ... plus = no longer

Je ne comprends rien.	= I understand nothing. (I don't understand anything.)

Here are some more useful negatives. These operate so that the second part (such as aucun, que) goes **after** the past participle.

ne ... aucun = no, not a
ne ... que = only
ne ... personne = nobody
ne ... ni ... ni = neither ... nor

Il n'a eu aucun problème.	= He had no problem.
Elle n'a payé que 10 euro.	= She only paid 10 euros.
Je n'ai vu personne.	= I saw nobody.
Il n'a mangé ni les bananes, ni les pommes.	= He ate neither the bananas nor the apples.

15 Imperatives

This is used to tell somebody what to do, as a request or an order. There are three forms:

i The 'vous' form; used to one person you do not know well, or two or more people.

ii The 'tu' form; used to one person you know well.

iii The 'nous' form; used to mean 'let's do something'.

How do I form the imperative?

a use the 'vous' form of the present tense and drop the vous.

Regardez! Ecoutez!	= Look! Listen!

b use the 'tu' form of the present tense and drop the tu.

Finis ton travail!	= Finish your work!

Note that with an ER verb, you must drop the final -s.

Regarde! Ecoute!	= Look! Listen!

c use the 'nous' form of the present tense and drop the nous.

Partons!	= Let's go!

What about the imperative with reflexive verbs?

You'll need a reflexive pronoun.

Levez-vous! Lève-toi! = Get up!

Note that **te** becomes **toi** in the imperative.

Watch out for these exceptions!

AVOIR	ETRE
(i) ayez = have	(i) soyez = be
(ii) aie = have	(ii) sois = be
(iii) ayons = let's have	(iii) soyons = let's be

16 Interrogatives

There are three ways to ask questions.

- Inversion (turning the subject and verb round) and add a hyphen. (Formal)
  Tu manges: Manges-tu?
  Tu as mangé: As-tu mangé?
  Il est parti: Est-il parti?
  Elle a mangé: A-t*-elle mangé? (* Put in the t between the vowels)
- A more informal way of asking a question. Use intonation (raising your voice at the end of the sentence).

Tu as fini.	= You have finished.
Tu as fini?	= Have you finished?

- Place Est-ce que / qu' ...? before a statement.

Il aime le foot. (statement)	= He likes football.
Est-ce qu'il aime le foot? (question)	= Does he like football?

Common question words (see Pronouns 9 on page 139).

Combien ... de ...?	= How much / How many ...?
Comment?	= How / What?
D'où?	= From where?
Où?	= Where?
Pourquoi?	= Why?
Quand?	= When?
Qui?	= Who?

Here are two more forms that must agree with the noun following.

Quel / Quelle / Quels / Quelles? = Which?
Que / Qu' ...? = What?

17 Passive Voice

This is used when the person or thing performing the action (the subject) is also at the receiving end of the action,

J'ai été mordu par le chien.	= I've been bitten by the dog.
Il a été blessé.	= He's been injured.

But note this example where the past participle agrees with the subject.

Elle a été blessée. = She's been injured.

How can I avoid the passive?

- Use 'on'.
  On a trouvé le chien. = The dog was found.
- Use an active verb.
  Un moustique l'a piquée. = A mosquito stung her.
- Use an impersonal verb.
  Il est interdit de stationner. = No parking.

Nouns

1 Gender

All nouns are either masculine or feminine (m. or f. in dictionaries). People's names usually take the gender you'd expect such as le père (m.), la mère (f.).

Some nouns are always masculine, whether the person is male or female, such as le médecin, le professeur (although you may hear la prof in conversation).

Typical masculine endings: -ier, -eau, -ment and -age.

Watch out for these exceptions!

le silence	le camion	un été
le million	le côté	

Typical feminine endings: -ade, -ance, -ence, -ière, -ille, -ine, -ion, -té and -tié.

Watch out for these exceptions!

la page	la plage	l'eau
la cage	une image	la peau

There are some nouns that have both a masculine and a feminine form, such as un acteur / une actrice, un ami / une amie.

BEWARE some words have two meanings.
Here are some of the most common.

le livre = the book	la livre = £ (sterling)
le manche = the handle	la Manche = the Channel
	la manche = the sleeve
le voile = the veil	la voile = the sail

2 Definite Article (the + noun)

Singular		Plural		
Masculine	Feminine	Masculine	Feminine	
le / l'	la / l'	les	les	= the
au / à l'	à la / à l'	aux	aux	= to the
du / de l'	de la / de l'	des	des	= of the

Note that French uses a definite article where there wouldn't be one in English.

- parts of the body.
  Elle a *les* yeux verts. = She has green eyes.
  Il s'est cassé *la* jambe. = He broke his leg.
- for nouns used in a general way.
  J'adore *le* fromage. = I love cheese.
- for languages, countries.
  J'aime *la* France. = I like France.
  J'aime étudier *le* français. = I like studying French(!).

3 Indefinite Article (a, some)

Singular			Plural		
Masc.	Fem.		Masc.	Fem.	
un	une	= a, an	des	des	= some, any

Remember that des becomes de if an adjective is used before a plural noun. For example: de grandes maisons.

Note these rules:

- use de / d' in a negative construction.
  Je n'ai pas d'argent. = I haven't any money.
- use the indefinite article in lists.
  J'ai acheté des fleurs, des chocolats et des souvenirs. = I've bought flowers, chocolates and souvenirs.

BUT do **not** use an indefinite article for jobs.

Mon père est médecin. = My father is a doctor.

4 Partitive Article (some, any)

Singular		Plural		
Masculine	Feminine	Masculine	Feminine	
du / de l'	de la / de l'	des	des	= some, any

- Use de l' in front of a masculine or feminine singular noun beginning with a vowel or an 'h', such as l'eau, l'hôtel.

du vin = some wine
de la viande = some meat
des fleurs = some flowers
beaucoup de vin = lots of wine
assez de fruits = enough fruit
trop de bruit = too much noise

5 Plurals

Don't forget to change the article and the noun for the plural forms.

le garçon: les garçons — la fille: les filles
un garçon: des garçons — une fille: des filles

Many nouns add **-s** to become plural (as above) but others change their ending.

-al: -aux — un cheval: des chevaux
au / -eu: -x — un oiseau: des oiseaux

-s, -x, or -z don't change in the plural.
le nez: les nez
le bras: les bras

Nouns ending in -ou add -s.
un trou: les trous

6 Possession

Remember that in French there's never an apostrophe to show that something belongs to somebody. Use de + name.

Le vélo de Paul. = Paul's bike.

Adjectives

1 Forming Adjectives

Adjectives change their spellings so that they agree with the noun in number (singular / plural) and gender (masculine / feminine).

How does an adjective agree?

Singular			Plural
Masculine	Action needed!	Feminine	Masculine / Feminine
petit	Add -e for feminine and -s for plural.	petit**e**	petit**s** / petit**es**
jeune	*Adjective ends in -e* Add -s for plural but no -e for feminine.	jeune	jeune**s** / jeune**s**
gris	*Adjective ends in -s* Add -e for feminine but no extra -s for masculine plural.	gris**e**	gris / gris**es**
premier	*Adjective ends in -ier* Add grave accent and -e in feminine singular, and -s in plural.	premi**è**r**e**	premier**s** / premi**è**r**es**
heureux	*Adjective ends in -eux* Change -x to -s in feminine before adding endings.	heureu**se**	heureux / heureu**ses**
actif	*Adjective ends in -f* Change -f to -v in feminine before adding endings.	acti**ve**	actif**s** / acti**ves**

Note that the following compound (two used together) adjectives do not agree with the noun:

une jupe bleu clair = a light blue skirt
une robe bleu marine = a navy blue dress
des baskets jaune pâle = some light yellow trainers
des baskets vert foncé = some dark green trainers

Common irregular adjectives to learn!

Singular		Plural	
Masculine	Feminine	Masculine	Feminine
ancien	ancienne	anciens	anciennes
beau (bel*)	belle	beaux	belles
blanc	blanche	blancs	blanches
bon	bonne	bons	bonnes
cher	chère	chers	chères
favori	favorite	favoris	favorites
faux	fausse	faux	fausses
frais	fraîche	frais	fraîches
gentil	gentille	gentils	gentilles
long	longue	longs	longues
neuf	neuve	neufs	neuves
nouveau (nouvel*)	nouvelle	nouveaux	nouvelles
public	publique	publics	publiques
secret	secrète	secrets	secrètes
vieux (vieil*)	vieille	vieux	vieilles

* These forms are used before masculine singular words beginning with a vowel or silent h: such as un vieil homme.

Where do I place the adjective?

Place these adjectives before the noun:

beau	grand	joli	petit
bon	gros	long	vieux
court	haut	mauvais	
gentil	jeune	meilleur	

Place other adjectives after the noun.

une vieille voiture française	= an old French car
le petit train jaune	= the little yellow train

Remember some adjectives can go before or after the noun and can change their meaning depending on their position. See propre (below).

ancien = former / old	
mon ancien collège	= my former (ex) school
un collège ancien	= an old school
cher = dear / expensive	
mon cher cousin	= my dear cousin
un pullover cher	= an expensive pullover
dernier = latest / last	
le dernier CD de Céline Dion	= Céline Dion's latest CD
la semaine dernière	= last week
grand = great / tall	
un grand homme	= a great man
un homme grand	= a tall man
propre = own / clean	
Elle a sa propre voiture.	= She's got her own car.
La voiture propre.	= The clean car.

2 Possessive Adjectives

These go in front of nouns to show who owns what!

Remember that the form you use depends not on the gender of the owner (the 'his' or 'hers') but on the gender of the thing they own (in these examples the brother and the car).

son frère (frère is masculine)	= his brother
son frère (frère is masculine)	= her brother
sa voiture (voiture is feminine)	= his car
sa voiture (voiture is feminine)	= her car

Singular		Plural	
Masculine	Feminine	Masculine / Feminine	
mon	ma (mon*)	mes	= my
ton	ta (ton*)	tes	= your
son	sa (son*)	ses	= his / her
notre	notre	nos	= our
votre	votre	vos	= your
leur	leur	leurs	= their

*Use before a singular feminine noun which begins with a vowel or silent h, such as son amie.

3 Demonstrative Adjectives

These are used before nouns and mean:
singular – this, that plural – these, those

Singular		Plural
Masculine	Feminine	Masculine / Feminine
ce, cet	cette	ces

cette femme	= this / that woman
ce stylo	= this / that pen
ces enfants	= these / those children

For emphasis you can add -ci or -là.

ce stylo-ci / -là	= this pen (here / there)

4 Comparatives (how to say something is more than something else)

- use plus before the French adjective to say 'more' or the 'er' form of the English adjective.

J'ai une plus grande chambre.	= I've got a bigger bedroom.

Comparing two things

aussi ... que = as ... as, moins ... que = less ... than
plus ... que = more than

Il est *plus* grand *que* sa soeur.	= He is taller / bigger than his sister.
Il est *moins* intelligent *que* sa soeur.	= He is less intelligent than his sister.
Elle est *aussi* gentille *que* son frère.	= She is as nice as her brother.

Note: Elle n'est pas *si gentille.*	= She is not as nice.

You should use si after a negative.

Note: use meilleur(e)(s) for better.

Comparing more than two things: superlatives

These are adjectives such as *the* best and *the* worst.

le plus / moins + masculine singular adjective
la plus / moins + feminine singular adjective
les plus / moins + masc. / fem. plural adjectives

Le train le plus rapide.	= The fastest train.
La chanson la plus célèbre.	= The most famous song.
bon = good	
le / la meilleur(e)	= the best
mauvais = bad	
le / la pire	= the worst
le / la plus mauvais(e)	
petit = small	
le / la plus petit(e)	= the smallest
le / la moindre	= the slightest

5 Indefinite Adjectives

autre(s) = other

les autres garçons	= the other boys
chaque = each	
chaque élève	= each pupil
même(s) = same	
la même trousse	= the same pencil case
les mêmes livres	= the same books

tout / **toute** / **tous** / **toutes** + article = all

tout le vin	= all the wine
toute la famille	= all the family
tous les livres	= all the books
toutes les fleurs	= all the flowers
plusieurs = several	
plusieurs livres	= several books
quelque(s) = some	
quelques garçons	= some boys (several)
tel / **telle** / **tels** / **telles** = such	
un tel homme	= such a man
une telle histoire	= such a story

Adverbs

Adverbs give us more information about verbs, such as well, slowly: She sings (verb) *well* (adverb); he walks (verb) *slowly* (adverb).

1 Formation

Simply use the feminine form of the adjective and add -ment.

heureuse: heureusement = happily

Watch out for these exceptions!

constamment = constantly	gentiment = nicely
énormément = enormously	mal = badly
évidemment = evidently	poliment = politely
précisément = precisely	
vraiment* = truly / really	

* If the masculine form of the adjective ends in i or u add -ment.

Normally, you put the adverb after the verb, but in the perfect tense the adverb nearly always goes between the auxiliary and the past participle.

Il a souvent parlé.	= He often talked.
Elle a trop mangé.	= She ate too much.

Adverbs of time go after the past participle. Examples of these are: tard = late, hier = yesterday.

Je suis arrivé hier.	= I arrived yesterday.

Watch out for these adverbs!

avec soin = carefully	tard = late
beaucoup = a lot	tôt = early
longtemps = for a long time	trop = too much
mal = badly	vite = quickly
mieux = better	

2 Comparatives and Superlatives

As with adjectives, use: plus = more, moins = less, aussi ... = as.

Il a marché aussi lentement que sa soeur.	= He walked as slowly as his sister.

Plus, moins or aussi go before the adverb whereas que follows the adverb.

The superlative of adverbs is formed by using le plus or le moins + the adverb. No agreements are necessary here as the superlative describes the action of the person not the person. Le plus therefore does not change to la plus or les plus.

Il conduit le plus vite.	= He drives the fastest.
Elle conduit le plus vite.	= She drives the fastest.

Remember that the adverb **bien** (= well)
becomes **mieux** (= better) and **le mieux** (= best).

Elle travaille le mieux.	= She works the best.

Pronouns

(words which stand in place of nouns)

1 Subject Pronouns

A subject pronoun tells you who or what is performing an action. Remember ils (they), is used for a mixed group, ie masculine + feminine nouns together.

Les garçons + les filles = ils

Ils vont au café.	= They are going to the café.

2 Direct Object Pronouns

A direct object is the person or the thing at the receiving end of the verb:

Il → subject, me → object, regarde. → verb = He is watching me.

Je mange **la pomme**.	= I eat **the apple**.
Je **la** mange.	= I eat it (*la* replaces *la pomme*).
Je ne la mange pas.	= I don't eat it.

The direct object pronoun goes before the verb and after the subject.

Preceding direct object + agreement

In the perfect tense, the direct object pronoun goes before the past participle and makes it agree. Add the agreements according to the gender of the direct object, not the gender of the subject.

J'ai mangé **la pomme**: Je **l'**ai mangé**e** (add -e).

J'ai acheté les pommes: Je **les** ai achet**ées** (add -es).

J'ai vu **le** garçon: Je **l'**ai vu (no agreement).

J'ai vu les garçons: Je les ai vu**s** (add -s).

3 Indirect Object Pronouns

These pronouns replace à + noun (to the boy – to him – lui). They are used with verbs which are followed by à:

demander à
dire à
offrir à
parler à
répondre à
ressembler à
téléphoner à

Il **m'**a demandé.	= He asked me. (to me)
Elle **lui** a dit que...	= She told **him** / **her** that... (to him / her)
Je **leur** ai offert un cadeau.	= I gave **them** a present. (to them)
Ils **lui** ont parlé.	= They spoke to **him** / **her.** (to him / her)
Elle **m'**a téléphoné.	= She phoned **me.** (to me)

4 En

This pronoun replaces a word which begins with du / de la / de l' / des (of it, of them, some, any, from it, from them). It goes before the verb.

Tu as **des stylos**?	
Oui, j'en ai deux.	= I've got two of **them**.
Tu veux **du fromage**?	
Oui j'**en** veux.	= I'd like **some**.

5 Y

Y means 'there' when referring to a place already mentioned. It replaces à + place.

Je vais **au café**.	
J'**y** vais.	= I go **there**.

6 Position of Pronouns

Generally, pronouns go before the verb, and in compound tenses (tenses such as the perfect, pluperfect) they go before the auxiliary verb. The exception to this rule is when you tell somebody what to do and use an imperative.

Regarde-la!	= Look at her.
Donnez-moi le stylo!	= Give me the pen.

Note that me and te become moi and toi in the Imperative. If you tell somebody *not* to do something then the pronoun goes in front of the verb and is in its usual form.

Ne **la** regarde pas!	= Don't look at her.
Ne **me** donnez pas le stylo!	= Don't give me the pen.

Order of Object Pronouns

If you use two or more, do so in this order:

Je la lui donne.	= I give it to her.

1 Subject Pronouns		**2** Direct Object Pronouns		**3** Indirect Object Pronouns	
je	I	me (m')	me	me (m')	of, to, for me
tu	you	te (t')	you	te (t')	of, to, for you
il	he	le (l')	him / it	lui	of, to, for himself
elle	she	la (l')	her / it	lui	of, to, for herself
on	one	se (s')	himself / herself / oneself	se (s')	of, to, for himself / herself / oneself
nous	we	nous	us	nous	of, to, for us
vous	you	vous	you	vous	of, to, for you
ils	they	les	them	leur	of, to, for them
elles	they	les	them	leur	of, to, for them

me				
te	le			
se	la	lui	y	en
nous	les	leur		
vous				

7 Emphatic Pronouns (stressed or disjunctive pronouns)

If you want to use a pronoun by itself such as it's **me**, some pronouns have special forms:

moi = me	nous = us
toi = you	vous = you
lui = him	eux = them
elle = her	elles = them

Use these:

- after prepositions: avec **moi** = with me
- if the pronoun stands by itself

  Qui l'a fait? **Moi**! = Who did it? Me!
- with même

  Je l'ai fait moi-même. = I did it myself.
- to emphasise subject pronouns

  Moi, je ne veux pas sortir. = I don't want to go out!

8 Relative Pronouns

- qui = who: used as the subject of a clause which follows:

  Le livre **qui** est sur la table. = The book **which** is on the table.

  subject noun + verb: use qui.

  La femme **qui** habite en face. = The lady **who** lives opposite.
- que = whom / who: used as the object of a clause which follows.

  Les sports **que** je préfère. = The sports which I prefer.

  object noun + subject + verb → use que
- dont = of which, of whom, whose

  Le disque **dont** je te parlais. = The record I was telling you about.

  La fille **dont** le père est professeur. = The girl whose father is a teacher.
- Lequel (m), laquelle (f), lesquels (mpl), lesquelles (fpl) = which: use these pronouns after prepositions such as avec and dans when you are referring to things, not people. (For people use à qui.)

Remember to choose the pronoun according to the gender of the thing to which you are referring.

Le stylo avec lequel j'écris. = The pen with which I write.

Note: If you link these words to à the form changes to: auquel, à laquelle, auxquels, auxquelles.

If you link these words to de the form changes to: duquel de laquelle desquels desquelles

9 Interrogative Pronouns

- Qui (subject) = Who? (talking about a person)

  Qui va en ville? / Qui est-ce qui va en ville? = Who is going into town?
- Qui (object) = who(m)?

  Qui est-ce que tu regardes? = Who(m) are you watching.
- Que (subject) = What? (talking about a thing)

  Qu'est-ce qui te surprend? = What surprises you?
- Que (object)

  Que fais-tu? / Qu'est-ce que tu fais? = What are you doing?
- (De) quoi = what?

  De quoi parles-tu? = What are talking about?
- Lequel / laquelle / lesquels / lesquelles = Which one(s)

  Laquelle des jupes est-ce que tu préfères? = Which one of the skirts do you prefer?

10 Demonstrative Pronouns

- ça / ce = this / that

  Regarde ça! = Look at that.

Note that ça is the shortened form of cela.

Note the use of cela.

Avez-vous vu cela (or ça)? = Have you seen that?

Going for an A?

- celui (m/sing), celle (f/sing) = this one, that one, the one which

  Quel livre?
  Celui qui est sur la table. = The one which is on the table.
  Celui-ci. = This one here.
  Quelle trousse?
  Celle qui est sur la table. = The one which is on the table.
  Celle-là. = That one there.
- ceux (mpl), celles (fpl) = those ones

  Quels livres?
  Ceux qui sont sur la table. = The ones which are on the table.
  Ceux-là. = Those ones there.
  Quelles trousses?
  Celles qui sont sur la table. = The ones which are on the table.
  Celles-ci. = These ones here.

11 Possessive Pronouns

	M Sing	Fem Sing	M Plural	Fem Plural
mine	le mien	la mienne	les miens	les miennes
yours	le tien	la tienne	les tiens	les tiennes
his	le sien	la sienne	les siens	les siennes
hers	le sien	la sienne	les siens	les siennes
ours	le nôtre	la nôtre	les nôtres	les nôtres
yours	le vôtre	la vôtre	les vôtres	les vôtres
theirs	le leur	la leur	les leurs	les leurs

The choice of form depends on the gender of the noun, not on the gender of the owner,

C'est la trousse de Paul.

C'est la sienne. = It's his.

12 Indefinite Pronouns

- **quelqu'un** = somebody

  Il y a quelqu'un dans la maison. = There is somebody in the house.

- autre, chacun, plusieurs, quelques-uns / quelques-unes, tout:

autre = other(s)

Où sont les autres? = Where are the others?

chacun / **chacune** = each (one)

Chacun des garçons, chacune des filles, chacun va payer. = Each one is going to pay.

n'importe qui = anybody

N'importe qui peut le faire. = Anybody can do it.

plusieurs = several

Tu as des CD?

Oui, j'en ai plusieurs. = I have several.

quelques-uns / **quelques-unes** = some (a few)

Quelques-uns des garçons sont gentils. = Some of the boys are nice.

Quelques-unes de ces assiettes sont sales. = Some of these plates are dirty.

tout = everything

Je veux tout faire. = I want to do everything.

Tout le monde est arrivé. = Everybody has arrived.

Index

Key: regular numbers (18) = Foundation,
italic numbers (*18*)= Higher,
bold numbers (**18**)= Word list

accommodation 24–27, *30–31*, **89–90**
activities 18–21, *22–23*, 40, 66–68, **82**, **85**, **86**, **88**
adjectives 135–137
adverbs 137
advertising 72–74
alphabet 7
animals **79**

bank 50, **99**

café 56–58, *62–63*, **100**
campsite 25, 33, **89**
careers 72, *75*, **104**
changing money / bank 50, **99**
chemist 8, **81**
cinema 18, **87**
clothes 49, *53–55*, 67, **98**
colours 7, 67, **79**
complaints 26, 49, *53*, 57, *62–63*
conditional tense *22*, *38*, 131
countries 33, **92**
coursework 3

days of week **108**
directions 40–41, **95**
doctor / dentist *9*, **80**, **104**

exam grades 2
exam technique 4–6

family 7, **79**
fashion 50, *53*, **98**
festivals / special occasions 33, *44*, *69*
food *15*, 56–58, *62–63*, **96–97**, **100–102**
furniture **82–83**
future tense *15*, 20, 35, **86**, **91**, **112**, 130

geographical surroundings 40–41, *44*, **94**, **95**
going out / invitations 18, 40, **87–88**
grammar 1, **109–112**, 127–140

health 8, *9–11*, **80**, **81**
holidays 24–27, *30–31*, *69*, **89–93**
booking in 24, 26–27
describing 33–35, *37–39*, **91**
problems *30–31*
hotel 24–27, *30*, **89**
home 12–14, **82–84**
household tasks 13, *16*, **82**, **84**

illnesses **80**
imperfect tense 130
instructions 4–5
international world **105–107**

leisure activities 18–21, *22–23*, **85–86**
letter writing 20, 24–27, *31*, 36
lost property *54*

mock exam 1, 114–126
listening 114–117
reading 120–124
speaking 118–119
writing 125–126
myself / yourself 111–12, *9–10*

nationalities 7, **93**
negatives *10*, *15*, *38*, *40*, 49, 56, 67, *69*, *71*, 73, *75*, 133
nouns 134–135
numbers 25, 40, 42, 49–50, 66, **108**

opinions 8, *10*, *15*, *22*, 35, *38*, 40, *44*, 58, *62*, 68, 72–73, *75*, **87**

perfect tense 14, **86**, **91**, **109**, 128–129
positives *15*, *38*, *40*, 49, 56, 67, *69*, *71*, 73, *75*, 133

post office 50, **99**
present tense **110–111**, 127
pronouns 138–140

quantities 48, *62*, **98**
questions (interrogatives) 134

reading 6
rooms 16, 24, **82–84**, **89**
routine 13–14, *15–16*, 66, **82**

school 66–68, *69–70*, **103**
shopping 47–51, *53–55*, **96–99**
clothes 49, *53*, **98**
food 46, 53, **96–98**
speaking 5

telephoning 50, *54*
television (genres) 19, **87**
tiers 2
time (telling) 13, 19, 25, 47, 113
time markers 14, 20, *37*
tourist information 36
tourist office *36*
town 35, 40–41, *44–45*, 47, **94**
transport
accident *44–45*
car / breakdown 41–42, *44–45*
metro / bus 41, **94**
train / station 41–42, **95**
travel *44*, 67, **94–95**

verbs 127–134
vocabulary learning 1, 2

weather 34, 42, *44*, **92**
work / jobs 72–74, *75–77*, **104**
world, environment **105–107**
writing 6

youth hostel 33, **90**